# LEARNING
# ON DEMAND

## How the Evolution of the Web Is Shaping the Future of Learning

By Reuben Tozman

ASTD
PRESS

16  15  14  13  12             1  2  3  4  5  6  7

**ASTD Press** is an internationally renowned source of insightful and practical information on workplace learning and performance topics, including training basics, evaluation and return-on-investment, instructional systems development, e-learning, leadership, and career development.

**Ordering information:** Books published by ASTD Press can be purchased by visiting ASTD's website at store.astd.org or by calling 800.628.2783 or 703.683.8100.

Library of Congress Control Number: 2012940625

ISBN-10: 1-56286-846-2
ISBN-13: 978-1-56286-846-8

**ASTD Press Editorial Staff:**

Director: Glenn Saltzman
Community of Practice Manager, Learning Technologies: Justin Brusino
Manager, ASTD Press: Ashley McDonald
Cover, Design, and Production: Lon Levy

Printed by Victor Graphics, Inc., Baltimore, MD, www.victorgraphics.com

# Contents

# Foreword

History has taught us that market economies are typically characterized by extended periods of stability occasionally punctuated by short unstable periods that stretch the economic envelope into a new topography.

Technologies such as the printing press and the steam engine were catalysts for previous economic discontinuities. Today, we find ourselves in the midst of a particularly prolonged—some argue permanent—period of instability as worldwide adoption of disruptive innovations such as the web browser, social media, and the smartphone have rapidly converged to create a global digital nervous system.

Over the past 20 years the web has evolved from being a read-only tool that people used to access information into a rip-remix-reload platform for collaborative co-creation. Evolving upon this web substrate, social media platforms have experienced unprecedented adoption rates on a global scale; and the reach of both the World Wide Web and the social-media platforms that ride upon it has been significantly amplified via the application of mobile technologies. In short, the very rapid convergence of these three technology vectors has permeated what we do socially, professionally, and educationally to such an extent that we have become oblivious to the profound changes it has brought to how we connect, communicate, coordinate, collaborate, and take collective action.

What we are witnessing during this tumultuous and transformational period in history is the accelerating co-evolution of society and technology. In today's digitally interconnected world, information is the currency, individuals are the transport mechanism, interaction is the transfer mechanism, and insight is the value added outcome. Today, as the world becomes more interconnected, instrumented, and intelligent, computers have migrated from being crunchers of information to optimize productivity to connectors of people to create value. Given this backdrop, we can begin to conceive this converged digital nervous system as a pervasive and expanding ecosystem whose central purpose is to facilitate collaborative learning, enable collective action, and encourage growth on both an economic and individual level. In short, the convergence of these three technology vectors has created a digital learning layer that blankets the planet.

An undergirding argument of *Learning on Demand* is that learning professionals must understand how to tune in to the evolving nature of this digital learning layer in the design, development, and distribution of content that drives organization performance. As learning professionals, we need to consider the opportunities and challenges we will face as the organizations we serve look to break the bounds of the traditional classroom by leveraging this near ubiquitous learning layer to engage a worldwide audience at a scale and price point that was inconceivable a decade ago.

In researching the behavior of organizations in adopting new technologies, Peter Drucker popularized the notion of the routinization trap: a pattern where organizations typically apply radically new technologies to automate existing business routines. In this book, Reuben makes the compelling case that the field of training and development has tended to use technology to service an old model of education: one that looks to digitize and automate the classroom delivery paradigm. He also argues—very accurately to my way of thinking—that we need a fundamental rethinking of how to leverage the digital learning layer to change the game in learning. To quote one of Gloria

Gery's always piercing insights, "We don't need new technology we just need new thinking."

In order to maintain relevance in a world where "business as usual" is rapidly evolving into "business unusual," Reuben suggests we must leverage this digital learning layer to support the fluidity with which people are learning while performing. Furthermore, he recommends that to continue to add value to the organizations that we serve, it is imperative that learning content no longer be segregated from the systems and technologies used by the rest of the business. As a result, learning professionals must immediately begin to explore how the learning layer can be leveraged to enhance people's productivity at work, rather than simply asking how it can be exploited to accelerate our ability to deliver instructional content outside the work context.

In this book Reuben has made a solid and substantive contribution in describing his vision of a world where learning truly does become "on demand." Beyond this compelling vision, he outlines a new design paradigm that emphasizes the need to focus not only on how content is designed but also how it is deployed and consumed. Furthermore, he describes in great detail the technologies that can be employed to realize this new design paradigm. In short, the work you hold in your hands not only makes the case for change to an "on demand" learning paradigm but also provides a clear road map for doing so.

In having read this work, your charge will be to apply what you have learned within your own organization to make Reuben's *Learning on Demand* vision the reality it deserves to become. In that charge I wish you all every success.

**Tony O'Driscoll**
Executive Director, Duke Corporate Education
2012

# Preface

As a child, I didn't grow up dreaming of becoming an instructional designer. I didn't even have an interest in working within the technology space. In fact, I didn't know what I wanted to do until after I started doing it and found that I was able to not only follow best practices but also to create my own best practices that worked. During the last decade or so, I have been working at a company that I began. It is based on a set of beliefs and practices that I used while working for others, which helped me rise to the top of every organization I worked for previously. The path I traveled to become an instructional designer did pass through a formal master's degree, which was the second master's degree I worked on. Most of my education before instructional design was focused in the arts, having done a degree in creative arts, then philosophy.

As a budding philosopher, I spent a lot of time looking at how people interact with the environment around them. I looked at how different people drew different meaning from the same object. I wrote about how people "experience" events and how the body processes memories. The shift from philosophy to instructional design was very natural for me because I had already spent a considerable amount of time looking at research around learning and the processes for learning.

I'm a big believer in the foundations of a specific art or science. In other words, if you want to become a really good dancer, you should probably study and master ballet, jazz ballet, ballroom, and so on, before you either invent a new dance or call yourself a dancer without affiliating yourself with any style. I believe in the foundations of an art and I am deeply committed to the foundations of instructional design. In large part, my inspiration for writing this book comes from a strong desire to raise the bar on the value instructional designers bring to the business table for their organizations. I desperately want to see instructional designers who are rooted in the value initially conceived for the job, working in a world connected through technology that has changed everything around us, and who are valued by others sitting at the table as well.

I was involved with the computer-based training industry early enough to watch the evolution from CD/DVD-based courses to Internet-based courses, mostly set up as websites and then finally to learning management systems taking over. I remember listening to industry thought leaders talk about "blended learning" once the virtual classroom technology had matured, passed early adoption, and become mainstream. I remember thinking to myself how "blended" became the silver bullet for every learning intervention needed. I was dumbfounded how quickly everyone talked about it, with old timers saying "It's not new," and yet during every sales call I was ever on, it seemed to get mentioned as though it were brand new and very necessary for survival. I remember equally the enthusiasm over the term "Learning 2.0" as a way to incorporate the use of social media into training plan design. I felt the same way as I did when "blended" was all the rage.

It occurred to me then as it occurs to me now that the formal aspects of my instructional design education, where research was paramount and you worked with evidence-based reports and studies to make decisions, was not and is not the norm in our industry. Even five years ago, when I attended conferences and every track spoke of social media, I would ask, "Where's the evidence?" The lack of evidence about social media's effectiveness in the learning space at the time was more a result of slow uptake on doing the research and less about social media's potential effectiveness if used appropriately. That being said, as an industry we seem all too willing to simply buy into the next big thing without the evidence or study to suggest how the next big thing can actually be helpful.

Over the years, I've learned that although I am a classically trained instructional designer, the training and development industry is rife with instructional designers who are working in the field without a formal education, with simply experience, talent, and a lot of hard work behind them. It is with these instructional designers in mind, along with all the classically trained and formal education instructional designers, that led me to write this book. It is a book about evolving the role of instructional design to be consistent with the evolutionary trends of technology itself, while growing from the same roots that define us as instructional designers to begin with.

At the end of the day, our role is to help connect people to the knowledge they require to learn and act differently than they do now. For many of us, our role includes a host of other tasks, such as project management, development, writing, and so on. However, if you are an instructional designer, your primary responsibility is to effect change in thinking, behaviors, or environment to achieve some end goal relevant to the individual or to the organization that employs the individual. This book is all about how to connect people to those things given the seemingly natural evolution technology has taken and the coevolution humanity is taking with technology.

I attend many learning conferences and I see many instructional designers trying to find a seat at the decision-making table of their organizations. Instructional designers—formally trained or otherwise—need to begin the journey of exploring the technology world outside of training and development if they want to be able to sit down at the decision table with leaders. Why? Because it is the job of every leader of every organization to run the most effective and efficient organization that they possibly can. Technology helps businesses find more effective and efficient ways of running their business. As the technology race heats up and more advances are made in shorter and shorter time spans, businesses need all the help they can get in leveraging the technology in ways that make the processing of their business as natural as possible. There is an incredible opportunity to be part of the conversation about how to leverage people and technology to make businesses better, faster, and more profitable, and instructional designers should be a part of that conversation.

This book was meant to introduce instructional designers to ideas, technologies, and thoughts not common in the conversations found in learning conferences. My inspiration is the opportunities I have witnessed firsthand when technology has been used in ways that seem like it was always part of the environment. I'm fascinated by how integral our pocket devices have become in our daily lives and how intelligent they seem to be. We're seeing businesses finding their way into our lives by simply being part of the device and again, allowing us to do what we do, just better, faster, cheaper. I love that I can go about my day and take care of my banking, my shopping, my networking, and so on—all from one central interface. That interface somehow becomes my unique interface for what is distinctly mine and over time gets more and more personalized.

It is space on this interface that businesses are fighting for. The trends that have made that interface so integral to my life are the same trends that instructional designers need to be aware of. I have spent the last 10 years of my career trying to advance the field of instructional design by speaking up at conferences and talking about technology. Over those 10 years I have become aware of so much; and I feel that if I can open just a couple of minds to the opportunity, then our field can evolve in leaps and bounds.

This book was also my opportunity to present a different vision for what learning systems could look like if they were built as an extension to the evolving technology around us. The vision presented unfolded mostly prior to the writing of the book itself, but was most certainly influenced by the people I interviewed, the articles I read, and the books I've referenced. In having conversations with people both inside and outside my industry, all of whom work with advanced technologies and all of whom believe in the principles of on-demand technology, I learned that I wasn't alone. I learned that the vision presented in this book isn't some far off imaginary system, but rather a system already in place to some degree in the technology we use every day. Like everything else, I suspect it will take some people a little bit longer to discover the opportunity that awaits us as instructional designers when we begin to engage with the technology as designers instead of just users. After all, we all use Internet search, a lot of us play games on the phone that connect us with our friends, we all have our remote support groups, and this connectedness and playfulness allows us to learn things and change how we interact with the world every single day.

I hope this book awakens a desire to connect with your instructional design roots. I hope this book gives you enough to think about so that you can join in the conversation about what systems we should be working toward and how we can best support the people in our organizations to do their jobs and learn in the most effective and efficient way possible. More so than anything, if this book encourages you to explore the outer edges of the technology world and what's possible, and you are able to bring some of that back to make you a better designer, then I will have done my job.

# Acknowledgments

Writing a book was very different than I had imagined it. I could never have made it through without the people who have influenced me, the people who supported me, and the people who actively helped me get this book together.

First and foremost, I thank my wife, Nancy, and my children, Zachary and Alyssa. There were many days and many evenings when they were patient and understanding when Daddy couldn't be there with them. My wife made the whole process of writing as easy as it could be by making sure all the duties I was neglecting were taken care of without a hassle. This could not have been more meaningful or important to me, and I am grateful to all of them.

Thank you, Aaron Silvers, and a special thank you to Cammy Bean. I'm not sure I could have written a book that made any sense to anybody but myself without the commitment from Cammy to edit, comment, and push me to be better when I thought it was as good as it was going to get. I thank you both for continually challenging me and influencing me in the best possible ways.

Finally, thank you to ASTD Press for giving this book a shot. Thanks to Justin Brusino, who believed in the concept and made this happen. And thanks to Alfred Imhoff, who took the time to understand what I was trying to say and edited the book in a way that really made it better.

Although Kevin Kelly will probably never read this book, his own book, *Out of Control,* was the single biggest influence on how I think about systems and how I make sense of the world. Thank you for the inspiration!

**Reuben Tozman**
2012

# Introduction

## How Is Web-Enabled Learning Like a Hockey Team?

---

As the World Wide Web evolves, web-enabled learning is also evolving. And this makes learning on demand via the web possible.

Learning on demand centers on a critical moment of need, when a person really wants knowledge about a specific topic to help them through that moment. It is the point at which an individual is unable to move forward until he or she gets answers, and the process whereby an individual obtains these answers is where he or she is literally learning on demand.

In contrast, most education in our schools and workplaces has been designed based on the principle of a preplanned activity, whereby a person is exposed to new knowledge regardless of his or her immediate needs. This static type of activity is typically called a push-based event, because information is pushed to an individual.

Learning on demand, on the other hand, is referred to as pulled learning because the information required is dynamically pulled by the individual. Learning on demand has always been around. Ever ask a fellow employee how to do something at work? Ever go to a library to find a book on building something around the house? We teach ourselves how to do things all the time, and we have always found the resources to help us with our individual projects and needs. Any time we take it upon ourselves to learn something new, we are learning on demand.

# The Birth of the Semantic Web

As the web continues to evolve, it has begun to become the semantic web, a term used to describe a future state of the Internet, when we will still be able to connect to the information and people that we do now, but when that same technology will make our task of finding what we need a lot easier. This evolution obviously has huge implications for learning, and that's what we'll be exploring in the chapters to come. Meanwhile, however, the Internet today is still a series of webpages that are assembled and packaged onto physical hardware. The hardware where the webpages sit is all physically connected through cables, switchboards, and various pieces of software that help computers speak to one another.

At this stage of the Internet, users are able to connect to information through links between webpages. One page has a link to another page, which has a link to another page, and on and on. But in the semantic web, the information on a page becomes connected to information on another page through a shared relationship of what the content actually means. For example, information on a webpage might contain the name of a Canadian province, and information on another page might also contain the name of a Canadian province. The semantic web will create a connection between the two webpages based on the common relationship of Canadian provinces each appearing on the page.

The connections between pieces of information on the web will be made for us, which will be different from today—when we, the users, jump around looking for pages that are connected based on our interests. Semantic web technology will make the Internet friendlier to use and will bring order to some of the chaos we currently experience.

I've written this book for my learning practitioner peers—the instructional designers, instructional developers, human performance technologists, and even thought leaders. The book presents a different model for learning based on the evolution of various types of technology related to the World Wide Web and the creatively disruptive force the web has been in other aspects of our lives.

From where we stand today, as learning practitioners, we have been quick to adopt new technologies, but we have been less enthusiastic about updating our training models. Our use of technology has been about bending the technology to service an outdated model of education. So, as I explain just below, my friend Kevin Thorn helped me to clarify the book's more technical aspects so those who don't have a deep technology background or expertise won't lose interest. Understanding the technology is crucial to taking advantage of what it can do for us, and crucial to ensure that our profession adapts to the disruptive forces of the web.

## The Hockey Analogy

While working with my friend Kevin Thorn on ideas for visualizing some of the more complex ideas in this book, we stumbled on an analogy that I believe captures the concepts, ideas, and suggestions contained in these pages: Learning programs are like hockey—they are complex, fast-moving, require close team coordination, and so on. This hockey analogy comes from the fact that I grew up in Montreal loving hockey, though a baseball or football analogy would also apply very well—as you will soon find out.

To make this hockey analogy work, let's start with a basic assumption: Our job as learning practitioners is to model content in the most effective way, to generate results that lead to learning and performance. On the topic of modeling content, consider Figure I-1, and imagine the content that we manipulate into learning programs as players on a professional hockey team.

**Figure I-1.** Imagining the Content of Learning Programs as Hockey Players

Now imagine that our job as learning practitioners is to create the ultimate hockey team to suit the different types of hockey enthusiasts—the fan, the coach, and the owner—as shown in Figure I-2.

**Figure I-2.** The Fan, the Coach, and the Owner

Each user has his or her own view of what the hockey team should look like. Of course, we are accustomed to designing our content with an audience in mind, and we do so based on the characteristics not only of the audience but also of the content. Likewise, in hockey, the characteristics of players—their height, weight, speed, skating proficiency, running proficiency, and jumping proficiency—make them more suitable for one position or another, though there are always exceptions. For example, a hockey defenseman, as shown in Figure I-3, should be larger in stature, and for him speed is not as important; he has long limbs, he uses a longer hockey stick, and he is strong.

**Figure I-3**. A Hockey Defenseman

As a designer of hockey teams, when I put together a team for a fan, if I want to make the game more exciting, I may create a team that is smaller in stature, faster, and more offensively minded, as shown in Figure I-4 by the more agile player.

**Figure I-4**. A More Agile Team Member

Thus, when designing a hockey team, I look at the fan's requirements and I assemble a team that targets his or her needs much the same way that

I do when designing a training program. For instance, to put together a team for a coach, I might choose to bring together a defensive team—one that has fewer goals scored against it, and whose coach can worry less. Of course, this team configuration is subject to the league in which the coach may play (that is, the training environment) and the coach's boss, the owner (project stakeholder group).

Moving our model for designing and assembling hockey teams into the future, imagine a pool of athletes who aren't designated as any player for any sport on any team. Each athlete has a set of attributes. As shown in Figure I-5, some are muscular, some are tall and lanky, some are small but fast, some have great hand-eye coordination—and the list goes on.

**Figure I-5.** A Pool of Athletes Not Designated as Players

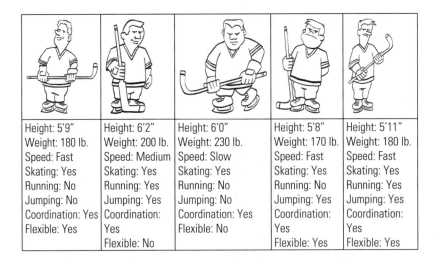

| Height: 5'9" | Height: 6'2" | Height: 6'0" | Height: 5'8" | Height: 5'11" |
|---|---|---|---|---|
| Weight: 180 lb. | Weight: 200 lb. | Weight: 230 lb. | Weight: 170 lb. | Weight: 180 lb. |
| Speed: Fast | Speed: Medium | Speed: Slow | Speed: Fast | Speed: Fast |
| Skating: Yes | Skating: Yes | Skating: Yes | Skating: Yes | Skating: Yes |
| Running: No | Running: Yes | Running: No | Running: No | Running: Yes |
| Jumping: No | Jumping: Yes | Jumping: No | Jumping: Yes | Jumping: Yes |
| Coordination: Yes | Coordination: Yes | Coordination: Yes | Coordination: Yes | Coordination: Yes |
| Flexible: Yes | Flexible: No | Flexible: No | Flexible: Yes | Flexible: Yes |

Imagine that this pool of athletes served as a common player pool for our hockey team as well as other hockey or professional sports teams of all kinds. Now consider if the hockey team's designer (the learning practitioner) put together a set of rules and player attributes for the type of hockey team that would be ideal for the team's owner:

- There is a total of six players.

- There is one goalie, there are two defensemen, and there are three forwards.

- The three forwards break down as center, left wing, and right wing.

- The two defensemen break down as left and right; but there is also one offensive defenseman and there is one defensive defenseman.

- The goalie should be medium height and strong but not overly muscular, have great hand-eye coordination, and be flexible and fast.

- The offensive defenseman should be medium height but muscular and strong, be fast, and have good hand-eye coordination.

- The defensive defenseman must be tall, have a muscular build, be slower footed, be physically strong, and not be afraid to battle for the puck.

- All the forwards are smaller and are fast, have short limbs, have great hand-eye coordination, and work well in teams.

In designing this ideal type of hockey team, if I were to follow today's common practice, I might use Google to search for these attributes to find links to the right players. If I pointed Google to our pool of players, it would display the search results ranked from more to less relevant. And as the designer, I would need to sift through these results and find the players according to where Google said they could be found. What if each player was accompanied by a sign that described all his attributes—as given below the picture in Figure I-6?

**Figure I-6.** A Player Wearing a Sign With His Attributes

Height: 6'0"
Weight: 230 lb.
Speed: Slow
Skating: Yes
Running: No
Jumping: No
Coordination: Yes
Flexible: No

And what if Google was such a sophisticated search engine that it could not only match words but actually understood the question? Today, when I query Google for "offensive defenseman," it doesn't understand that I'm only looking for a defenseman who is offensively minded. It simply goes out and matches the words "offensive defenseman" with its set of built-in heuristics. But imagine if it actually did understand the question, "Who are the best offensive defensemen?"

For Google to understand a question like this, there would need to be a common, consistent framework for discussing those attributes that apply to all players. In other words, "height, "weight," "leg length," "arm length," "speed," and so on would form a common language that could be used to discuss all the players. And there would also need to be a consistent format for representing the values for each category of attributes. For example, height is measured in feet and inches, and weight is measured in pounds. Having a consistent way to categorize and describe the players would help Google understand the similarities and differences, and would also help the designer to set parameters for the design of our hockey team.

This process of constructing a common language whose variations are expressed in a consistent format is *normalization*. Normalization, in our analogy, is the creation of a consistent set of attributes and values that we attribute to all players, as shown in Figure I-7. To normalize content is simply to create the attributes and values for tagging the content. Remember the signs under the players giving their attributes? That's tagging.

**Figure I-7.** Normalized Attributes and Values

| Height: 5'9" | Height: 6'2" | Height: 6'0" | Height: 5'8" | Height: 5'11" |
|---|---|---|---|---|
| Weight: 180 lb. | Weight: 200 lb. | Weight: 230 lb. | Weight: 170 lb. | Weight: 180 lb. |
| Speed: Fast | Speed: Medium | Speed: Slow | Speed: Fast | Speed: Fast |
| Skating: Yes | Skating: Yes | Skating: Yes | Skating: Yes | Skating: Yes |
| Running: No | Running: Yes | Running: No | Running: No | Running: Yes |
| Jumping: No | Jumping: Yes | Jumping: No | Jumping: Yes | Jumping: Yes |
| Coordination: Yes | Coordination: Yes | Coordination: Yes | Coordination: Yes | Coordination: Yes |
| Flexible: Yes | Flexible: No | Flexible: No | Flexible: Yes | Flexible: Yes |

The actual ways in which the players mix and pursue the game together are determined by the rules of the game. We choose the types of players for our team based on the game they are going to play. Likewise, when we design content for training, we may configure the same piece of content in various ways, depending on how the content is being deployed. For example, when we build software training, we tend to design content as simulations and animations that give a learner the opportunity to practice. Often these will include scenarios to help set context. However, the same content for executing a software task could easily feed a one-page support tool that simply contains the steps for how to execute the task, without the scenario and without the movement and interaction.

Ready to stretch your imagination? Imagine an intelligent hockey stadium (Figure I-8)—one equipped with computer processors and that has been programmed with the rules of hockey, that knows its different user groups (the fans, the coach, and the owner), and that is able to access a remote group of athletes, all of whom were tagged with attributes. In essence, then, this intelligent stadium is a very large computer that can even identify a particular fan who walks in—just as your room in one of today's technologically advanced hotels senses when you enter and switches on the lights for you.

**Figure I-8.** The Intelligent Stadium

Moreover, the intelligent stadium is networked and thus can access the pool of hockey players—if and when it is called upon to do so. In our analogy, the stadium would access the remote pool of players when a fan (that is, a user of the learning program) walked into the stadium, and from this pool it would match the attributes of possible players with the user's needs and then assemble the most exciting team. Then, as the fan sits ready to watch the hockey game, the stadium would deploy this team to provide the fan with the ultimate hockey experience.

# How the Analogy Clarifies Web-Enabled Learning

Now let's relate this hockey analogy to training. The stadium stands for our learning-on-demand system. The players stand for pieces of content—all with identifiable attributes and relationships. And the fan stands for the end user of our learning programs.

The future state of learning will be to enable our learning-on-demand system to understand the needs of its users, to pull from a remote pool of content the information that a user needs given her particular context, and then to use the rules around the environment (the game of hockey) to deploy the content. Many of you may think of this as performance support, and therefore as only a fraction of what the training and development world needs. But this book argues that everything we think of as training and development ought to be placed under the banner of performance support, and that this support is ultimately part of a business's operations.

As Erik Brynjolfsson and Andrew McAfee explain in *Race Against the Machine* (2011), computers are beginning to think for us by:

---

... doing many things that used to be the domain of people only. The pace and scale of this encroachment into human skills is relatively recent and has profound economic implications. Perhaps the most important of these is that while digital progress grows the overall economic pie, it can do so while leaving some people, or even a lot of them, worse off. . . . But . . . when we look at the full impact of computers and networks, now and in the future, we are very optimistic indeed. These tools are greatly improving our world and our lives, and will continue to do so. We are strong digital optimists, and we want to convince you to be one, too.

---

To relate the hockey analogy to current training practice, the learning practitioner today manually assembles a hockey team to give fans the best experience. With every new fan, and every new stadium, the learning practitioner places new players together, and thus facilitates a new experience. But when the learning practitioner works in the future state, what new skills will he or she need?

If this hockey analogy makes sense to you, then you're ready for the future of learning. The future of learning—the future for the "fans," the "coach," the "owner," and the "learners"—is to walk into the "stadium" and have it know what experience to supply. In the future, the World Wide Web—displayed on one's computer, mobile phone, tablet, or other device—will provide the learner with the best possible learning experience, tailored to his particular circumstances and environment.

# What's Next?

This book appeals to instructional designers at all levels to break out of our existing models for design and development. These models were built to service singular solutions. But now technology has given us an incredible opportunity to service the learning experience in all its multifariousness—providing individualized, learner-tailored answers, not one solution—within the context of performance. Thus, in this book you will explore emerging trends in the World Wide Web's technology by considering the works of established thought leaders and examples of technology trends in action. The book focuses on the trends in innovation inside training and development departments and discusses how these trends are simply a regurgitation of well-worn academic design strategies. They evince a resistance to how the web wants to evolve in keeping with how we can learn most effectively.

Where the web has already penetrated our lives, our learning processes are physiologically the same but methodologically different. The web has firmly entrenched an on-demand, fluid expectation for content, yet training organizations still limit their use of the web to simply embellish static events and solutions. Where the web has made the lines between personal life and business life almost obsolete, training organizations strive to stand out as a means of survival.

As the web continues to break down barriers as it evolves—and thus change how we interact with content, with each other, and with industry—understanding how to tune in to its evolving nature will be the key to designing and developing content that drives effective performance. In the next five chapters, you will learn design techniques that are consistent with the web's emerging trends that focus on helping the web understand the content you develop:

- Chapter 1 explores the foundational topics of supply chain management, how to manage the creative process in which instructional designers are always engaged, and how to leverage technology—all in the crucial context of the emerging semantic stage of the web's evolution.

- Chapter 2 delineates the new imperative for instructional design that is being driven by the key principles of evolving web technology—highlighting those aspects of the web's development that are pushing designers to constantly innovate.

- Chapter 3 introduces the reader to the new technologies that are being used for learning on demand and gives examples of particular tools and activities that use them to build a better platform for learning on demand.

- Chapter 4 presents a practical, detailed vision for what a learning-on-demand structure looks like that leverages the new web technologies.

- Chapter 5 focuses on the key skills for instructional designers—those you may well already possess, and those you may need to develop further—as well as practical tips and tricks for designing content, and a wrap-up of the book's lessons.

- The appendix provides case studies of actual new technology systems in action.

# Chapter 1
## Training With the Evolving Semantic Web

 **In this chapter, you'll learn about**

- How to master key foundational skills like supply chain management
- How to manage the creative process and leverage technology
- The semantic web and the web's evolution

What do instructional designers need to know about the business world to succeed in today's extremely fast-changing corporate environment? Even though the content of work is evolving at a searing pace, many of its basic principles are still the same, and thus designers need to master key foundational skills like supply chain management, how to manage the creative process in which they are always engaged, and how to leverage technology. This chapter explores these and other topics, and also introduces the semantic web in detail. But first, I will set the stage with the tale of a seminal experience that for me embodies all these topics.

## From Student to Project Boss

There I was, sitting in the back of a sport utility vehicle with five other people, only two of whom I had met previously. My stomach was in knots. I was about to be paraded in front of the top learning brass of a large grocery chain as a Montreal multimedia consulting firm's "instructional designer."

The vice president of this firm, whom I had just met earlier that morning, had submitted a proposal on a computer-based training initiative and had won the bid. The firm's proposal included the involvement of an instructional designer, about which they knew very little. So began their journey as an "e-learning company" that was frantically reaching out to find out what an "instructional designer" was. In their grasping, they connected with a friend of mine, who in turn gave them my contact information, and so began my journey as an instructional designer.

At the time, I was a graduate student in educational technology, one year into the program, and I was looking for real-life experience. And boy, did I get it: Within one eight-hour workday, I was transformed from a student into a full-time instructional designer, a project manager, and a production manager. And my ride in the sport utility vehicle turned out to be nowhere near as surreal as waiting to meet the learning brass from the grocery chain—only to see one of my professors leaving the meeting room with the same people I was seeing. I was competing with my professor for this project.

The next evening, the professor told our class the story of meeting me and spoke about the dangers of the grocery chain project for which we were both competing. He talked of scope creep, unclear objectives, and other nonsense that I would reflect on two years later—as the project was collapsing. By that time, a project that had been scheduled and budgeted for three months was two years in the making, and the client was still not happy. Who was to blame? Me.

I say "me," but I realize that my boss was also surely to blame because he had put me in the position where I could single-handedly influence a project to the degree that I did. I often debate with industry peers on the challenge of an instructional designer also serving as project manager. The nexus of my argument against this doubling of roles can be found in my first experience doing just that. Many of you reading this book are probably managing projects and also doing both the instructional design and the development in your organizations. Many of you would probably disagree with me that instructional designers shouldn't double-time on project management. The debate is a worthy one to have—but not here.

As both the instructional designer and overall manager for the grocery chain project, I pushed the boundaries of the digital learning experience for my client, asking my team of graphic designers and programmers to build games and simulations. And nobody at my consulting firm reined me in. The grocery chain wanted an instructional designer to drive, and I was let loose. My designs dictated the project's scope and had an impact on the bottom line in ways with which I was then unfamiliar. Although the team must have questioned how the firm was ever going to make money, how could they argue? I was the instructional designer.

Two and a half years went by, and we delivered a product that had gone over budget by about two years' worth of work. But I did learn quite a bit from this experience—along with others, serving as an executive director, product manager, and consultant—about supply chain management, about managing the creative process in which instructional designers are always engaged, and about leveraging technology.

# Supply Chain Management: Not as Boring as It Sounds

Supply chain management is an important concept for instructional designers to learn. If we look closely at the time and the cost required to design and develop off-the-shelf e-learning versus custom e-learning, we can learn a lot about the concept of supply chain management. For this comparison, assume that the quality resulting from both types of e-learning is the same. What is it about building off-the-shelf versus custom e-learning that makes the former more efficient? Why are the design and development of an off-the-shelf product faster and less costly than a custom course?

The idea that off-the-shelf production is a more efficient and cheaper process than custom development applies almost universally across industries. Think of making yourself a table from scratch versus producing huge quantities of tables for others. What would you do to make the process more efficient? You'd probably start by buying tools to make your work easier and more efficient. You'd use the tools to shape the wood, assemble it, and move the finished tables. But at some point, you'd look at how to automate some or all of the process so machines could do the heavy lifting, so to speak. Yet before you brought in the machines to automate the process, you'd need to create a template of what the table was going to look like and adjust the machines to recreate your template over and over. Likewise, e-learning can in essence be mass-produced. For instance, as a product manager for an e-learning vendor, I managed a team of resources dedicated to building a library of off-the-shelf e-learning courses. Having only managed the design and development of custom e-learning in the past, I was amazed at the productivity of a small team of qualified people—and it was all in the supply chain management.

Our product already had a look and feel. Our product already had canned exercises and assessments that were applied to content. Most important, our designers knew what activity types to apply to which types of content. There was a high degree of predictability in our process, and a lot of the creativity that consumes resources in a custom build was set aside. Some of the activity types we built into our courses were automated, but we hadn't really figured out a machine to completely automate the process.

The one element that really made the difference was the structure that was given to the instructional designers in the off-the-shelf courseware development team—not the technical structure but the instructional design structure that mapped how to treat content with similar learning objectives with the same limitations and opportunities inherent in the product. The instructional designers who were assigned to design the content analyzed the raw content, associated learning and performance objectives with this content, and then mapped the content on the basis of their learning objectives and performance objectives to the feature set of the product.

If I were to distill what worked with the off-the-shelf course that would also work with custom e-learning, I would propose the following:

- Find a cognitive theory or model that fits with the bulk of our work.

- Market to our clients that we subscribe to this theory and that there is academic evidence to support the theory's viability.

- For each "category" within the cognitive model we've chosen, build out a series of web screens that are mapped to the learning category.

- Show how each screen uniquely addresses the expected learning outcomes of the learning category. In other words, what the learner does on-screen accurately reflects the behaviors expected from the level or category within the cognitive model.

- Use these screens as a selling point to demonstrate an ability to produce large volumes of content for our clients in a predictable, understandable way.

- Allow our clients to brand or customize the look of every screen, but ensure that the screens remain the same programmatically.

- Shift our instructional design process to be more of an information-mapping process than a free-flowing, creative process.

- Always allow for the instructional designer to break out of the mold if required.

These steps can be followed or adapted in other situations where you want to be able to mass-produce content. Let's look at an example of how this can work. Company ABC is about to launch a new product, and so the top managers decide to train its sales force to be able to explain the benefits and features of the product versus those of its closest competitors. Company ABC would like the training to focus on handling objections because it has set its strategy to go after its competitor's clients.

Imagine being part of a custom e-learning design and development shop, where most of your projects deal with product sales. You have therefore identified common learning objectives and performance objectives that seem to apply to most of your client's projects, regardless of product and even client:

- The learner is able to demonstrate active listening by repeating questions back to prospects when asked.

- The learner is able to list the benefits and features of the product when asked by a prospect.

- The learner is able to successfully pair client's needs with the right product.

The process of grouping similar learning and performance objectives together into generic objectives is essentially the building of a cognitive model. Using the cognitive model in this example, I have identified the following online activities that help learners achieve these goals:

- Play an audio file and the learner must identify key points that were present in the audio file.

- Create a list by selecting items from a larger pool of items based on a question asked by a prospect.

- Match product features with a list of needs.

For each of the activities, I have created a variety of sample web screens for each activity that I can show a client:

- Option 1: Uses talking avatars and a text box.
  Option 2: Static images with audio file and text box.

- Option 1: Game-like interface with a timer.
  Option 2: Drag-and-drop interface.

- Option 1: Drag-and-drop interface using text only.
  Option 2: Drag-and-drop interface using a combination of audio and text.

There are fundamental differences between the approach laid out here and a traditional approach to the custom design and development of e-learning. The essence of these differences is the separation of the instructional approach to fulfill the learning and performance objectives with how this approach looks and feels on a computer screen. It's the identification of elements that support learning regardless of the look and feel. For an example from another part of the computer world, see the sidebar.

The process for the cognitive model of learning is not radically different from the object-oriented programming model for software development, whereby data used by software are not hard-coded into the functions of the software.

# Managing the Creative Process by Leveraging Technology

To an instructional designer, the thought of automating the creative process of developing an online course seems unreasonable. I agree. I'm certainly not trying to remove the instructional designer from the design and development of e-learning. But I am trying to reorient the skills an instructional designer requires in the future. Web applications are becoming increasingly powerful. They know who we are (Facebook), they know where we are (Global Positioning System), and they will know what content we need and when. This is the essence of the World Wide Web 3.0—again, known as the semantic web, which is explained in more detail below.

To return to the hockey analogy, as was explained in the introduction, web 3.0 is our "intelligent hockey stadium." For instance, instead of following the conventional custom e-learning design and development process (which treats individual pieces of content one at a time), or using templates in a simplistic fashion, the semantic web makes possible a much more dynamic, responsive experience. The templates that designers work with today contain standardized functionality, with a look and feel that can be adapted. Thus, because the functionality is already locked, designers are left to stuff content into a template that may or may not have the elements needed to support the learning experience.

For example, far too many online courses use an assessment with a multiple choice or true/false format at the end of the course, regardless of the subject. Why? Because multiple choice questions are easy in all respects, and there are tons of available templates. Nonetheless, most instructional designers would agree that in many cases the multiple choice format is completely inappropriate for the level of assessment required.

Multiple choice questions test a learner's ability to recognize the right answer. A multiple choice test does not assess the learner's ability to execute a task, solve a problem, or perform other higher-order thinking skills. All instructional designers know this, but we use these tests anyway and try our best to write "good" ones. However, when we recognize that multiple choice questions are an inappropriate format for the level of assessment we're trying to implement, we are recognizing that, structurally, this type of test does not have the elements required to support our targeted learning experience.

When I proposed a new approach for the custom design and development of e-learning to my boss at the time, my idea was to instantiate things like multiple choice as part of a cognitive model where "identification of the right answer" was the learning experience. This approach would find success by streamlining the storyboarding process as well as the production of a course. Storyboarding is no longer a page-by-page creative process. It is a process of moving raw content into a cognitive model based on its associated learning and performance objective. The cognitive model dictates the elements of design for an instructional designer. The time and effort needed for development are significantly reduced by limiting custom programming and streamlining quality assurance testing.

In chapter 5, we'll thoroughly explore this process, which requires new types of skills from the instructional designer. Throughout this book, I seek to show why these skills are important for an instructional designer, who will use them in a world where technology can automate much of the manual labor of assembling courses.

# The Semantic Web and the Web's Evolution

It just so happens that what makes supply chain management so efficient for e-learning is also what makes a semantic web possible—structure! In his book, *Weaving the Web* (1999), Tim Berners-Lee sets the stage:

I have a dream for the Web [in which computers] become capable of analyzing all the data on the Web—the content, links, and transactions between people and computers. A "Semantic Web," which should make this possible, has yet to emerge, but when it does, the day-to-day mechanisms of trade, bureaucracy and our daily lives will be handled by machines talking to machines. The "intelligent agents" people have touted for ages will finally materialize.

The web in its earliest form was always conceived of as network of hyperlinked information, where information was grouped, tagged, and accessible through other information. "He was certain that every document in the world should be a footnote to some other document, and computers could make the links between them visible and permanent" (Kelly, 2005). As the web evolves into this, it has on its path digressed, but slow and steady it is coming around. We began with web 1.0, are now in web 2.0, and are forging ahead to web 3.0.

Web 1.0 could be defined simply as an interactive and visual web, its defining service being the search feature; while web 2.0 evolved into a programmable web, characterized mostly by a sense of community, through the use of blogs and eventually social networks. While web 2.0 is essentially an array of applications and social media tools, web 3.0 is more of a concept of how the Internet should work and is mostly commonly referred to as the semantic web. Contrary to some perceptions, web 3.0 is not a replacement for web 2.0, but rather an evolution of it. Web 3.0 can be defined as representing a range of Internet-based services and technologies that make data more understandable to machines, and by doing so makes information easier to find and more understandable to people (ASTD, 2011).

Web 3.0, the semantic web, is the bookmark that will start the era when the web achieves its initial vision, and is still—according to many experts—far away into the future. Rest assured though, that the web is moving in this direction and there are many trends that support this.

While the web surges forward and grows into what it was meant to be, it seems as if it is sweeping everybody and everything into it. Some people, media outlets, and self-publicized thought leaders even discuss that as the human race evolves, its evolution is directly entwined with the evolution of the web, so much so, that the web appears as an extension to our own evolution. We see the reflection of this evolution with almost everything we create today. We put chips into everything so that we can communicate with inanimate objects. We integrate the web into our entertainment, communications, business, and family. We extend ourselves and all of our relationships into the web and create avatars of ourselves. Our digital selves talk with, share with, and interact with a world of other digital people who we've never met outside the web. We've even changed how we speak to each other outside of the web to accommodate new protocols founded through communication over the web. We have commerce, virtual worlds, and programs that are beginning to understand "natural language." And thus the semantic web will be able to understand the difference between:

- Fred saw a plane flying over Zurich.

- Fred saw a mountain flying over Zurich.

The semantic web understands that mountains can't fly, and therefore it inherently understands the second sentence as Fred was flying over Zurich when he saw a mountain. And therefore, if you use the semantic web and reference this sentence, it will know whether what you are referencing makes sense within the meaning of the content and will disregard all non-sensical inferences.

It is not surprising, then, that almost all industries are evolving to incorporate the web into its natural order of things. There are two general ways in which industry does this. The first way is to use the web in some capacity to streamline its own business. And the second way is to plug into the web along with its customers. Using the web for businesses used to mean setting up an online store where goods and services can be purchased. This has evolved into complex marketing campaigns where consumers are able to interact with the organization itself. It is about the experience and the engagement that come from the participation. Consider Jell-O brand's latest marketing campaign, the Jell-O mood meter. The mood meter is a live read of the Twitterverse scanning for emoticons depicting smiles and frowns. When the

Twitterverse trends toward frowning, the Jell-O mood meter visually shows a frowning face and begins sending Twitter followers a link to free pudding. The fascinating part to this for me is the automation. A web application completely left alone analyzes real-time data and interacts with virtual people all on its own. In addition, the virtual people who represent real people engage with a web application—in a somewhat stinted conversation, but a conversation nonetheless. Man is conversing with machine.

With respect to improving one's own business processes by webifying them, consider that more and more commerce is now being done over the web, along with marketing, accounting, and project management. Companies are restructuring based on mobile workforces, tapping into talent across oceans, providing local service through international offices, and harnessing consumer trends like never before. However, it is true that you can't turn a culture that is not social in nature into a social culture by implementing tools (Bozarth, 2011). We are nonetheless seeing an evolution in social cultures through tools and the evolution of tools through social cultures.

Our evolution as a society is deeply entangled with the evolution of web technology. We have moved beyond building tools to help us communicate; we have built tools that are in return building us! The language that was at one point reserved solely for chatting with someone online is making its way into face-to-face conversations. Our online language allows us to express ideas and emotions differently. A great example of this is a hashtag I've seen in Twitter a lot, "#fail." This hashtag is used as a comedic expression of having messed up. For example, "Just finished building a deck in back. Looks horrible. #fail." It's not uncommon now to hear people say out loud "hashtag fail" to bring a comedic sigh of relief to a potentially stressful situation. The story of web technology is no longer only about tools to help us do something better. It's a story of coevolution, whereby technology and society are inter-dependent. Web technology breaks down the lines between work and play, family time, and work time. It is as though the technology is grafted into our lives in an intelligent way so that our use of it is seamless. We don't have to stop doing what we're doing to use the technology. We use it as part of our lives—as we use it, it also evolves.

Imagine that we could apply this model to training. Imagine using technology to enhance our productivity at work rather than stopping our work to consume training content. Imagine that content is built into our environment through technology. We are at this point. Technology can help us create self-organizing groups, learning on demand, and a networked system that interfaces with all facets of the organizations where we work. To accept this promise is to accept a radical shift to the paradigm of training and development. It is a shift that will entail re-engineering and reconfiguring the training function, as part of operations or even marketing, to ensure that it is better supporting the business. This new view of training, however, is based on established systemic approaches; for an example, see the sidebar.

## The Dick and Carey Systems Approach

Walter Dick and Lou Carey's Systems Approach Model for instructional design—initially published in 1978, and presented very eloquently in their 1996 book *The Systematic Design of Instruction*—set out a very simple yet elegant process for designing training or education. The model is based on a process of analysis, design, development, implementation, and evaluation (ADDIE). The ADDIE model is a difficult model to discredit since it has a very common sense approach and is an established business analysis model. In essence, the approach states that before you can develop a solution to a problem or to meet a goal, you need to understand the need. Once you have a good understanding of the need or requirement you can design the solution without spending the dollars to actually have it developed. Once it's developed you can implement it and then evaluate it for success. Over the years the model has seen refinement; it has evolved to suit rapid prototyping and remains a fixture in the instructional design landscape. It is the model on which most instructional designers create online learning.

I am a believer in Dick and Carey. I believe we need to look at our requirements, and look at our needs based on the five tenets for the web's will to create a new design imperative. Dick and Carey didn't create their model at a time when the world's collective intelligence was online and on demand!

Observing our use of the web disrupts some of the assumptions we've made in training over time. The web has shown us and has proven that learners are able to close knowledge and skill gaps themselves. People are able to search for and retrieve the information they need to move from *I can't do it* to *I can do it* without any sort of formal process being in place that's controlled by an expert. To a small degree, we accommodate some self-directed training in our conventional training delivery model through what we call *performance support*. Performance support used in conventional contexts is simply a side note. It is something to accompany training, not to replace training itself. Part of the issue is in our preconceptions about the limitations in self-directed learning and how we define a "moment of need."

Self-directed learning is not something that we typically reserve for "learners" who are new to a subject or skill. Our theory is that novice learners don't know what they don't know, so how could they direct their own learning? A person who is being introduced to a subject or skill needs the right foundation, the right scaffolding to help them build the mental models, and skill sets to become proficient. This is our conventional wisdom. In chapter 4, I introduce Sugata Mitra's Hole-in-the-Wall experiments, which demonstrate that learners with no previous background in a given subject are able to acquire 30 percent of what they would need to pass a test without any formal solution or initiative at all. These are learners who don't know what they don't know. Add in some facilitation into the mix—not formal education per se, but some degree of facilitation, with subject matter being acquired through self-directed learning—and the results are even more convincing.

I am not trying to say that learning doesn't need scaffolding. I am questioning conventional wisdom about a person's ability to create his own scaffolding. I also question our definition for "the moment of need." We typically reserve this moment of time to discuss when somebody is actually in the process of doing something, acting on, researching, and so on. We would rarely if ever use this to capture moments such as "first week on the job." First week on the job is just too vague to lump into a moment of need. It is because we think of training as an event as opposed to a fluid stream of experiences or activities that limits our use of moment of need. In fact, from a common sense perspective, when would we do training at a corporate level outside a moment of need? Isn't that like saying, you don't really need this, but here it is?

When we apply Dick and Carey's model to the corporate training world, we end up talking a lot about competencies. The needs gathering stage identifies learners and environment but a big slice of the analysis is generally around what a worker needs to know and do after training. The assumption we all take for granted is that the training is the event to close the gap between unable to perform and successful performance. There is also a belief that closing the gap happens during training and the reinforcement happens on the job. We currently design our training materials based on the assumption that we need to deliver the learning itself. Our deliverables need to be packaged nicely, and must contain the bridge that walks a person's mind and body from *I can't do it* to *I can do it.* We have always assumed that the instructional designer controls this by doing the needs analysis, uncovering the gap, and then designing and developing ways to bridge the gap.

It is the premise of this book that training and development needs to better leverage technology to serve a new and constantly evolving model of education and not fall behind the times. As a result, innovation within training and development needs to find ways to build tools that facilitate this new model. Thus, innovation in training and development needs to become more in tune with the web's natural evolution elsewhere. For more perspectives on the web's evolution, see the sidebar.

## Perspectives on the Web's Evolution

The evolution of the web has been characterized differently by different people at different times. For instance, Kevin Kelly—one of the founders of *Wired* magazine, a known "futurist," and a recognized researcher of web trends—presented the web's evolution in a series of talks. In his TED talk "Predicting the Next 5,000 Days of the Web" (2007), he discussed how the web has moved from sharing packets to linking pages and is now heading toward linking data. Sharing of packets is when an Internet user manually shares a packet of information with another user, not unlike faxing something to somebody.

The web in its current form is in the "linking of pages" phase. Internet users no longer have to manually send packets to other users to share information, they can put up a page and others can link to it. The web contains trillions of links and exchanges terabytes of data per second, all working through pages that are linked to one another.

In the third stage of the web, data are linked to data through a shared relationship that web applications can understand. Pages linked to other pages have links that physically appear in the page itself. This is what allows a web user to move from one page to the other. The content within a page is irrelevant to our current web applications. Future web applications will be able to link pages together for users based on the web application's ability to draw relationships between the content itself, thus linking data to data. The link between data is found in the meaning of the content.

For example, Montreal and Toronto are both Canadian cities. In a web that links data to data, a relationship is drawn between these two pieces of data by web applications through a variety of mechanisms that help the application understand the relationship. I discuss these technologies at length in chapter 3. Ultimately, a web application would be able to determine that both are cities and that both are Canadian, and that they are in adjacent provinces.

The shift required in training and development is innovation supporting the fluidity with which people are learning while performing. Most of us don't naturally learn from 1 p.m. to 2:30 p.m., but learn through the infusion of experience followed by repeated cycles of experience and reflection. Where the experience begins and ends is different for everybody, and reflection on experience is a mixture of personal baggage with the contents of the experience.

Given that learning in a corporation is used to support performance, why isn't training a tool in the performance support utility belt, instead of performance support being a tool in the training utility belt? Consider an example that explains this situation and how it might change. A very large, influential Canadian government corporation has a well-established training and development department, which spends all its efforts designing training solutions that include all the greatest hits—classroom, e-learning, job aids, online synchronous. Another important department is engineering, which is responsible for the efficiency of the plants and equipment. The corporation, though profitable, was not meeting its own service levels, and so it asked its training and engineering departments to find out why.

As consultants hired by the training department, my colleague and I focused our investigation on the tools in place to ensure that the folks in the plants were performing to full potential. We found there really were no consistent descriptions to enable the firm to define and measure job-ready resources, the skills required, and performance levels.

For instance, when we broached the measurement issue with engineering, we were told of a department made up of 350 people who stared at computer screens, looking at the real-time data flashing and scrolling past. As these data flashed on the computer screen, the employees looked for data patterns. The data were being sent to these monitors from the actual equipment in the plants—from retail outlets, human resources systems, and all other kinds of systems. The data appearing on the monitors were apparently so rich that the person speaking with us described how they caught an employee stealing from them simply by tracing data patterns of time, place, and product type.

As data passed on the screen, those reading them and finding patterns were able to pinpoint machines, people, and processes that were not working according to standard operating procedures. They were able to identify a problem with machine x, in location y, and based on the patterns determine human error, machine error, or other error types. When human error was recognized, somebody from the team was dispatched to the location to meet with the person causing the error and regulate the issue. The person sent out to solve the problem was highly skilled and knowledgeable about the standard operating procedures and corporate standards and coached the individual on exactly what they needed as determined by the data received.

What makes this scenario so fascinating? First, the training department knew that this was going on, but it didn't interface with this group nearly as much as it should have. Second, all learning systems would have shown the people in their jobs as having learned the content and therefore being job ready. Yet the engineering systems were very clearly showing different data. I would also argue that the data coming out of engineering were simply more critical to the business than the training data. Do we need to ask ourselves why training is siloed? Thus, this example demonstrates the clear divide between *learning* and *performance*.

My experience working with this organization reinforced the need for training and development staff members to plug into what makes a business tick. Instead of only focusing on individuals, training and development teams must learn how an organization's systems function, and must also develop new analytical models rather than the ones we have used for learning.

# Chapter 2
## Toward a New Design Imperative
## for Web-Based Learning

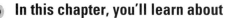 **In this chapter, you'll learn about**

- The web's two core aspects and five distinctive characteristics
- How each of the five characteristics applies to training and development
- The principles for designing materials for the evolving, viral semantic web

---

This chapter explores a new design imperative based on key principles of web-driven technology. Every medium used to communicate with learners imposes a set of advantages and limitations that both help and hinder the designer in his or her work. The print medium is portable, provides a blank canvas to visually communicate, and merges formatting with the meaning of content. However, content in print cannot be easily updated, is not linkable, and limits the size of the visual canvas. And there are other qualities of print that designers must work around when required. Optimizing communication in print requires a designer to work with the medium and within its limitations.

In much the same way as when instructional designers work with a print medium, the medium of the World Wide Web demands that they work in specific ways. Materials delivered in print demand that content is structured and formatted as it would appear to the reader. The print environment demands that the meaning of what is being written is consistent with and sometimes explained through its formatting. For example, when you see: "I am really angry" on a page, it visually conveys something different from: "I AM REALLY ANGRY!"

When designing materials for a classroom session, an instructional designer needs to create specific materials—for example, the designer of a printed participant's manual needs to set up a clearly decipherable table of contents. Instructional designers who design for print are also instructional developers: They need to master language, syntax, vocabulary, and communication theory. Those designers who are working with print thus need specific skills to ensure success.

Likewise, instructional designers who work on the web need particular kinds of skills. These skills range from layout design to usability design, and this raises several key questions about what constitutes effective design on the web:

- When is it best to use audio?

- How can you best display large volumes of text?

- If you encounter low bandwidth requirements, how do you design good interactivity?

We'll be considering how you can best answer these and many other related questions in the chapters to come. But in this chapter, I seek to set the stage for a new design imperative for developing web-based learning. We'll look at the core web characteristics that resemble what would otherwise be called a will. To appreciate this new design imperative, building on the story of the web's evolution told in chapter 1, I highlight those aspects of the web's development that have really pushed the web to what it is today and those that are pushing it to what it is becoming.

# The Web's Two Core Aspects and Five Distinctive Characteristics

The two core aspects of the web that are driving its evolution and its ability to alter the way we design and consume learning are 1) its ability to share and 2) the cloud. Although the initial vision of the web was a web of hyper-linked data, a distributed network that could carry information even during a nuclear attack (see reference below), somewhere in the web's evolution sharing, collaboration, and community became central features. Where some may have dismissed these aspects of the web in early 2000s as silly (I was one of them), there is no denying the impact of the social media venue in web reality today. This phenomenon is now a critical aspect to the web and in itself is a fundamental contributor to the ongoing evolution of the web. In this chapter, I show that the relationship between how data are now linked and will be linked in the future, though unpredictable, is in fact interdependent with the rise of social media.

The other core aspect of the web and its evolution is the cloud. Very briefly, the cloud is the notion of content and data living in the hosted network we call the Internet. When people speak of the cloud, they are referring to the digital world accessible through their web browsers and web applications.

Currently, the cloud refers more to an IT infrastructure, but its power as a concept is much more significant. The notion of some ethereal body of content, services, and products, from which the entire planet shares, isn't just about linking pages or data. It's the idea of a single repository where everyone contributes, plays, works, and learns. The cloud is the ultimate icon for hive mentality. The reward is that the collection is greater than the sum of its parts.

Within these two core aspects of the web, five distinctive characteristics have been and will continue to be instrumental in the web's evolution:

- The web needs to be fed.

- The web wants to understand what it is being fed.

- The web wants to be viral.

- The web wants you to use it very personally.

- The web wants you to communicate with others.

The training and development community was using computers as early as 1960 with the ideas of enabling computers to complement the education system and of delivering education sessions to learners through the computer. Although the earliest systems were networked, their purpose was to substitute the teacher–student experience with a computerized version. In other words, it was a replacement for a teacher, designed to deliver education to a student in the same way a teacher would.

The first major computer-based education system was Programmed Logic for Automated Teaching Operations (PLATO), which was developed in 1960 at the University of Illinois. By 1976, PLATO had already grown up to include personal notes, chat rooms, instant messaging, and monitor mode, which was remote screen sharing. PLATO became the model for other systems, which we now call learning management systems.

What if we superimpose the web's will into our practice? Just as paper to some degree dictates how to design training materials, the web surely does as well. So how does the web change how we design materials? What does it mean to design materials that feed the web, allow the web to understand them, are viral, want you to use the web very personally, and allow for communication?

## The Web Wants to Be Fed

Again, in edging into this topic, I beg your indulgence for a personal story that sets the stage. When I first started using the web back in the mid-1990s, the most fascinating thing for me was not its content but its infrastructure. It was the ability to remotely hook my computer up with another computer that was additionally shared by others who were all hooking in. Taking part in synchronous chats and meeting people was far more meaningful than any of the conversations I was actually having. Telnet was all the rage. There was no content and if there was, there was no browser to look at it. Then I blinked.

I opened my eyes to a whole new world where I could see satellite images of the world. There was a browser where I could type in some cryptic code named a URL and my window would show me a real-time live view of the Earth from space. Then I blinked again and opened my eyes to find that I could type in a URL to something called AltaVista and Yahoo. I could type in things I wanted to find and rather suddenly I was learning about things using my browser's search. Then I blinked with the rest of the world and we opened our eyes to find this thing called the World Wide Web, which quickly became a hub for communicating, researching, and entertaining.

Between the time I began studying educational technology and the day I landed my first job, the field of instructional design had gone from designing computer-based training discs to designing web-based learning. That was a period of three years. In three years the web was suddenly able to handle heavy media files. The infrastructure itself was changing underground and the software for compressing media was changing above ground. The explosion of content that has manifested in the web is simply inconceivable considering the business model for doing so simply didn't exist as it was all happening. Value on the market as we are taught in university level economics is based on scarcity, among other things. Posting content on the web for free seems completely counterintuitive based on a value model of scarcity. Releasing a free chat service on the web that requires you to share it for it to become valuable was so against the grain of best business practice, it's hard to even express. Yet when ICQ (AOL Messenger) was first released for free by Mirabilis (the Israeli company that built it), it seemed to have immediate value. It left people scratching their heads about how this company was ever going to make money, but that didn't deter them from using it and increasing the value of the software simply by sharing it. If you're having a hard time understanding value, Mirabilis sold ICQ to AOL on June 8, 1998, for $407 million.

ICQ was brilliant. It had no value at all if you were the only person who had it. You needed to share it for it to become valuable to you. As more people received the tool, more people needed to share it for it to be valuable for them. Suddenly the value to AOL was that millions of computer users had this software program on their computer. It was a window to deliver content to these users at a magnitude unheard of before. Suddenly there was a new model for value.

Mirabilis wasn't the first company to give their software away for free. Linux is one of the most successful open source platforms to date. IBM began investing in Linux in 1999. Open source platforms or software are developed for free by a group of individuals within a single organization or from different organizations. The platforms or software is free to use and free to alter, but with a caveat that any modifications or alterations must be fed back to the open source group and neither the modifications, nor your instance of the software, can be sold for monetary rewards. Linux has spawned some incredibly innovative ideas, products, and services that not only create value for them but also increase the value of Linux itself.

If we look at IBM's model for deploying Linux as open source software, supported through its global business services, we get a sense of the value proposition for feeding the web. Feeding the web through contributions such as content, products, and services is all about strengthening the network. It's about building value in the network rather than a single identity. The story of ICQ is a great example of the value that can be gained by contributing to the web. By contributing to the web, you are sharing, and in doing so, you prompt others to share. And in prompting others to share, everyone who has shared benefits. This is building strength in the network. It is the increase in value the network has for those who are part of it, both monetarily and pragmatically.

For the web to survive, it requires constant feeding. For the web to be valuable to us, it needs to grow. And to grow, it needs us. Stagnation would be the end to the web. For those who don't contribute to the web, the value proposition back isn't anywhere near what it could be. User-generated content is something of a new phenomenon and provides the basis for how the web exploded. We didn't always have blogs and wikis, but the web has always had contributors trying to build the value of the network through contributions to the network. As the network's value grew, it presented an increasing pool of opportunities for individuals and businesses to operate.

How does all this apply to your work as an instructional designer? The materials that feed the web insinuate designing content to strengthen the network. When we discussed feeding the web, the value in doing so was to increase the network's value. We have always designed materials targeted to our profiled learners, and have implemented training consistently with their environment, but we have never really considered how to help our learners by adding value to the network that supports them day in and day out. Web technology is so pervasive in all businesses that even a closed networked system is still a web-based system. An organization's network includes one that supports sales, human resources, marketing, operations, and any other formal and informal strategic business units. Consider materials that add value to this network.

It is no longer enough to design training materials that have a singular purpose. To design materials that strengthen the network, you need to

- create materials that not only help the targeted audience but can also be used by other members of an organization

- create materials that draw links to other resources on the network.

Think back to the discussion about value and how to establish value on the web. Think about how you can weave what you're doing into the network, and you will increase the value of your materials.

## The Web Wants to Understand What It Is Being Fed

The web is either a single chaotic mess or a series of interconnected patterns. What side of the fence do you sit on? It was probably not too long ago, where the pendulum might have swung to the side of pure chaos. More and more though, the web is becoming that series of patterns resulting in a more usable system. The web is also becoming more understandable to itself. The notion of a web that understands itself comes from Tim Berners-Lee's vision for the semantic web, which we encountered in chapter 1. Although the semantic web that Berners-Lee envisioned may never happen, there is no doubt that content curation, natural language reasoning engines, semantic searches, and other terms relevant for a semantic web are finding their way into our lexicon (for definitions of these and other related terms, see, for example, www.quora.com/web-content-curation and www.netlingo.com/dictionary/c.php).

As humans have done throughout history, we classify, categorize, and name things. We organize our own digital lives in digital folders, and businesses organize their lives in digital folders—and as the repository of digital things becomes larger, classifying and categorizing things becomes more difficult. This constitutes the problem of big data, which is the term used to describe the overwhelming quantity of information gathered by our software programs and analytical tools that were initially designed to help us make better decisions. Big data also refer to the overwhelming amount of data and content accessible to us through our search engines, web applications, and software programs. The amount of data and content that are generated on a consistent basis and made available to us exceeds our ability to consume and analyze it. To illustrate this: Mankind created approximately 150 exabytes (one billion gigabytes) of data in 2005. In 2010 it created 1,200 exabytes.

Merely keeping up with this flood, and storing the bits that might be useful, is difficult enough (IBM, 2010a). And from a business perspective, it is estimated that 80 percent of a company's data is unstructured data, making it difficult to manage and interpret for business use (*The Economist*, 2010b). This problem is the problem of big data.

Many of us spend two hours a day trying to find the folder where we've stored our digital files, according to information obtained from edCetra Training. We search for its title, its date of creation, its author, or whatever else we think of that may help us find it. Part of the problem is that the computer we're using doesn't really know what it is looking for, since it doesn't know the contents within the files. Another part of the problem is that the search engines don't understand the meaning of what we're asking for. It is simply trying to match words with words. The bigger problem is that our content is stored in folders (and potentially multiple folders) since a single file can't be shared among many folders.

This represents a real problem since we have multiple versions of a single file stored in multiple locations. Take our problem global and you can see that as the content stored in the web increases exponentially, the web's survival as a usable system depends on its ability to find us the content within it. The solution is to ensure that the web, as it plays out in various applications, can draw its own associations and relationships vis-à-vis content so that instructional designers can make the maximum use of it. As one observer concerned with our design challenge puts it, "Our job today and tomorrow isn't to organize ourselves better; it's to get the right technologies that respond to our personal productivity needs. It's not that we're becoming too dependent on our technologies to organize us; it's that we haven't become dependent enough" (Schrage, 2012).

Currently, the use of tags, hashtags, metadata, and others are the ways in which we have made content more understandable to the web applications we use. If we look at the history of the "#" hashtag used by the Twitterverse, we see the value a web application has when it can make sense of its own content. The twitter hashtag was born on August 23, 2007 (Gannes, 2010), and was used in the following way: "How do you feel about using # (pound) for groups. As in #barcamp [msg]?"

This tweet gave rise to a fundamental instrument for Twitter users to make the Twitterverse easier to navigate. It allows Twitter applications to filter through messages that share a common hashtag. A message marked with a hashtag lets the web know that it is an organizing principle with which to filter and organize information. There is no file system that keeps the messages stored. There is simply a relationship between random pockets of information that a computer program can understand marked by a simple symbol: "#." In 2010, Twitter averaged 50 million tweets per day. In June 2011, the average number was up to 200 million tweets per day; that's one billion every five days. The messages crossing through the cloud are as diverse as the people sending them, yet the use of a "#" symbol allows the cloud to parse through the messages in seconds and return to the Twitter user an organized stream of tweets per # topic.

There are no rules for using the hashtag. There are no predefined hashtag groups. If there were predefined hashtag groups, the value of the hashtag would probably drop pretty quickly. It's the crowdsourced relationships that are created by the free form hashtag that creates the value for users to add the hashtag to what they write. If you want in on the conversation, just pop in the hashtag code. In relation to hashtags, the W3C (www.w3.org) defines the vision for the semantic web as follows:

The vision of the Semantic Web is to extend principles of the Web from documents to data. Data should be accessed using the general Web architecture using, e.g., URIs; data should be related to one another just as documents (or portions of documents) are already. This also means creation of a common framework that allows data to be shared and reused across application, enterprise, and community boundaries, to be processed automatically by tools as well as manually, including revealing possible new relationships among pieces of data (W3C, 2012).

Thus, the key to the semantic web is about managing data through relationships, using a common framework shared by individuals, businesses, developers, and the like—think hashtag; that is, the # example ties together the semantic web and the idea of a common framework. As it stands today, there are many standards and many organizations managing standards, all trying to establish themselves as the common framework for linking data. The reality of the semantic web relies on the implementation of a single standard that can ultimately reason with all the other standards to normalize the variety of formats. Now remember those normalized tags for the hockey team discussed in the introduction (recapped as Figure 2-1)?

As our own evolution and that of the web become increasingly intertwined, accomplishing this feat is ultimately what the web wants from us and what we need from the web. A web that understands itself is able to process information at speeds unimaginable to us. Having the web process information also means that it can use the information and that we can

**Figure 2-1.** Recap of the Characteristics of a Pool of Athletes
Not Designated as Players

| | | | | |
|---|---|---|---|---|
| Height: 5'9" | Height: 6'2" | Height: 6'0" | Height: 5'8" | Height: 5'11" |
| Weight: 180 lb. | Weight: 200 lb. | Weight: 230 lb. | Weight: 170 lb. | Weight: 180 lb. |
| Speed: Fast | Speed: Medium | Speed: Slow | Speed: Fast | Speed: Fast |
| Skating: Yes | Skating: Yes | Skating: Yes | Skating: Yes | Skating: Yes |
| Running: No | Running: Yes | Running: No | Running: No | Running: Yes |
| Jumping: No | Jumping: Yes | Jumping: No | Jumping: Yes | Jumping: Yes |
| Coordination: Yes | Coordination: Yes | Coordination: Yes | Coordination: Yes | Coordination: Yes |
| Flexible: Yes | Flexible: No | Flexible: No | Flexible: Yes | Flexible: Yes |

develop learning programs, products, and services based on the web's ability to understand, process, and use information.

As the web becomes better at understanding and organizing content through standards, the instructional design community stands to provide their audience with more integrated learning experiences. A web that can organize content and understand who it's for, and its context, has much to offer the learning community when it comes to real-time, personalized learning.

Again, how does all this apply to your work as an instructional designer? If we are to design materials that are understood by the web, we need to look at the technologies we use to build materials. More elementary than this, however, is simply the notion of building materials in a way where there is an explicit relationship between various pieces of content or courses that can be used during the implementation of learning. It will still be a long time coming, and it may never happen that organizations feel more comfortable exposing content to the web at large. The notion of allowing the web to understand materials is limited in organizations that are more cautious about exposing its contents to the web at large. The task then becomes having an organization's network understand its own materials. At this level, designing learning materials is also designing the architecture of how the learning materials piece together to form a fluid experience for the learner.

Technology can facilitate this—if you investigate hard enough. But before you adopt the technology that will help you with this:

- You need to have it planned out.

- You need to start mapping out relationships and building content management strategies that you can employ through technology.

- You need to pursue data modeling at the instructional design level as one way to do the mapping.

We will cover data modeling extensively in chapter 5, but for a quick overview of the process, see the sidebar, *Data Modeling*.

## The Web Wants to Be Viral

At the age of seven, a Canadian girl began posting YouTube videos of herself performing cover songs from famous artists. With her 72nd posting, a cover of Lady Gaga's song "Born This Way," Maria Aragon got to experience why viral is so valuable. Lady Gaga herself heard the cover and tweeted the link to view Maria's video. Shortly after Lady Gaga's posting, Maria's video had been viewed 25 million times—and a new star was born.

Maria's story is one of many, where value (the ability to reap monetary rewards, fame, and influence) is driven through viral. It's not just content that increases in value when it goes viral, but also the web itself as an evolving organism depends on content going viral. The web's growth as an organic evolving system can be attributed in part by the viral phenomenon. You could say the web went viral!

# Data Modeling

Data modeling is "a process used to define and analyze data requirements needed to support the business processes within the scope of
corresponding information systems in organizations" (Wikipedia). By
building yourself a data model about how the disparate pieces of learning materials coalesce, you are a step closer to building a fluid learning
experience for the learner. Here's an example of a simple data model:

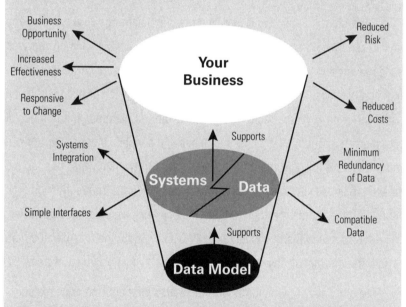

*Source: Wikipedia, http://commons.wikimedia.org/wiki/File:3-4_Data_model_
roles.jpg.*

If you eliminate the need for content on the web to be viral, then you remove what the web is surging toward. In fact, one could make the argument that to measure value on the web you must look at "web traffic" but you must also look at whether there is sharing—and how much sharing, how often, and by whom. Traffic alone used to be a significant metric for determining the value of an Internet property. Today, if that property isn't being shared, then you would need to question its value. If feeding the web was about building value in the network, then having what you feed the web going viral is the closing, and perpetuation of that loop.

There are really two ways in which the web facilitates viral content. The first is simply a passive link phenomenon, where a link existing on the web suddenly attracts the attention of thousands or millions of netizens, spawning emails, blogs, and tweets pointing others to the link. For instance, if you use Twitter or any other social networking tool, think about the number of messages that are links to other webpages and people's blogs. I can think of more than one link I've received through social networking that has led me to add the linked site to my repertoire of websites that I frequently look at. If others felt the same way, then through the one link passing through a variety of networks, the website has increased in value. Again the use of value here is no different than a conventional use of value; it's just arrived at differently.

The other way in which the web facilitates viral content is by making it possible to create a business model such as Hotmail that includes the necessity to share. Hotmail, before being taken over by Microsoft, would by default add a one-liner to all messages sent including a hyperlink for others to download Hotmail when sending emails. There was a purposeful intention to generate sharing.

Again, how does all this apply to your work as an instructional designer? Learning materials that are viral are shared. They initiate discussion, result in reflection, and lead to a deeper level of understanding. Learning materials that are viral create value outside the materials themselves. To make learning materials viral, you need to

- Allow the learner to contribute back into the repository of organizational memory—through, for example, cogent comments online, or by editing a Wikipedia page.

- Don't rely on a single channel from above to deliver your message.

- Design a fluid learning experience consistent with the web, which means allowing a flow back into the learning materials from the learners themselves, and then allowing learners to share and self-organize.

Conversations are naturally viral and have been a primary source for learning since humankind began communicating. Conversations spread ideas and help evolve and perfect the idea. Designing learning that is viral means including conversations and allowing for organizational memory to evolve and perfect itself.

## The Web Wants You to Use It Very Personally

As the web evolves to a more semantic, relationship-based network, it wants you to make use of it in a very personal way. Perhaps one of the biggest surprises to Internet aficionados was the willingness of people to turn their private life very public. In the late 1990s and the early 2000s, there was nothing within the web to really suggest that people would provide personal information about themselves in the way that they have since. As one expert put it, "Everything media experts knew about audiences—and they knew a lot—confirmed the focus group belief that audiences would never get off their butts and start making their own entertainment" (Kelly, 2005).

Sure, the idea of networking was latent in the web, but not necessarily the exposure. The use of social media sites to broadcast elements of one's personal life is where the web widened its scope away from merely being a network of hyperlinks to being what it is today. In retrospect, the collision between the exposure of one's personal life with a semantic web seems almost inevitable. As the web evolves to understand itself, and the more the web can understand content relationships and make use of who you are, the more valuable the web can become to you since its key organizational principles can be your profile.

Some of you are probably worried about a wide range of privacy issues that surface almost every day from known web giants—Facebook comes to mind. There is no doubt that privacy is an issue that needs to stay on all our agendas. Privacy violations are serious and I know more than a handful of people that choose not to share personal information on the web. For them the web remains only an infrastructure to collect emails and search for information. The truth is that the web has become so sophisticated that simply searching for something on Google tells the web analytics running behind Google a whole lot about who you are. As long as that information is being used to provide better service, and expand products and services that meet the needs of the Internet community, then the little bit of privacy you give up is worth it. It is also important to remember that the value you can derive from the web increases the more the web applications you use know you.

With so many of us putting so much information into the web, the sheer volume of information has gotten almost unwieldy (remember: one billion tweets every five days). So how can we make sense of what's out there and find what we want to know?

I've discussed how the web is evolving to understand what it is being fed through content based on relationships as opposed to pure indexing and filing. This is the way in which the web will survive. It is the only way the web will continue making sense given its exponential growth. Some of the relationships that the web wants to associate content with is who and what context is affiliated with the content. When web applications can assess this they can feed that information to other web applications, allowing the network of web applications to learn and evolve. As data is gathered about who is using the content and in what context, the data feed back to the web applications and allow them to provide better and better service. It is here where we see the true coevolution of the web with the evolution of humanity. Not only will the web evolve through its ability to establish context for content based on its relationships with people, but people will evolve through their ability to create personal experiences through the web that links them to content, people, and services. These experiences will feed a constant stream of analytics and derived meaning, and will be accessible through that same stream. To make the web manageable, we need to use it very personally, and the web needs us to use it very personally so that it can also provide an idiosyncratic experience.

A personalized, idiosyncratic experience is the holy grail of learning. As individuals constantly observing, reflecting, and learning, we all come into a learning experience with a variety of biases, opinions, cultures, and knowledge. As our education systems have evolved out of a home-based system, to a community-based system, and now to a global system, finding learning opportunities that match our specific context is rare, yet something we all crave. The notion of a personalized learning experience is the idea of a learning experience that accounts for you as the individual and accounts for your background, previous knowledge, context, and other important data points. It evokes your emotions and memories as well as your logical powers and curiosity. It is an experience rooted in an external goal that has been adapted and continues to adapt as you move through the learning experience as a unique individual.

Sam Quayle (2011) wrote in *Smashing Magazine* that "web gurus and industry analysts are simultaneously arriving at the same conclusion: We are entering a new chapter in the evolution of the web. Many would argue that the future of the web will be influenced by the growth of the mobile market and location services, and their beliefs would be correct. Both of these, however, are pieces of the bigger picture: personalization, instant data, and real-time communication."

A slightly different take on this article might be personalization through instant data and real-time communication. The whole notion of personalization is only achievable if you expose yourself. The importance of instant data and real-time communication is the ability to accommodate a web that changes and expands exponentially day to day and still achieves the personalization experience. This means that the experience you would get today would be different tomorrow and vastly different months from now. Personalization is only achievable through instant data and real-time communication, whereby you meet your exact need just when it is motivating you.

Again, how does all this apply to your work as an instructional designer? Take these steps:

- During the data modeling process, incorporating what you know about the audience is critical.

- Map out what parts of your materials are more appropriate for which audience types. What content is more suited for audience characteristics (for example, geographic location)?

- Create this map for yourself, and use it when the environment changes and specific elements of the content therefore need to change.

Having a map may help when other groups within the organization need material and they possess some of the same characteristics as your first audience. As organizations evolve to cloud-based architectures, having mapped audience characteristics into the context of materials will help cloud technologies operate naturally.

## The Web Wants You to Communicate With Others

The web wants you to communicate, with it and through it, with others. Communication makes the web viral. The World Wide Web is a global machine, to which there are no restrictions on who can use it. Posting or sharing anything on the web is an act of communication. Additionally, the reach of the web and the infrastructure that supports the web is so ingrained in us that it has become the backbone for how conventional communication utilities provide their services. The telephone industry is a great example of leveraging the web to improve services. Voice over Internet Protocol (VoIP) is a popular service that came on the market in 2004 and has since taken over roles in traditional telephony infrastructures to help reduce operating costs. Mobile telephone communication goes through the Internet backbone, and the conversion from traditional switchboard telephony to VoIP is increasing. In other words, the web was built to support communication.

Consider all the channels the web offers to those who wish to communicate. Whether for personal reasons, social reasons, or business reasons, the web offers a wide spectrum of opportunities to deliver your message and of course, to deliver your message to the right people. The spring of 2011, now named the "Arab Spring," was an incredible story of how the web was used for mass communication for social issues. TG Daily, an online magazine, had this headline in September 2011: "Arab Spring Really Was Social Media Revolution." The Arab Spring was the caption used to gift wrap the series of protests erupting in the Middle East, where ordinary citizens gathered to overthrow current rulers branded by mainstream media as despots. Whether the rulers of the Middle Eastern countries that were overthrown were despots or not is not an argument for this book (and probably not an argument anyone would take up). What is relevant is the utility of social media for the revolutionaries to post messages, pictures, and videos as a means of communication in real time. From a Western perspective, social media networks were far more revealing than what traditional media was able to report, to the extent that traditional media turned to social media channels to get their news.

And one final time, how does all this apply to your work as an instructional designer? The intent and act of training and education is of itself a form of communication. At its very core the design of learning materials should be consistent with all other channels of communication, so that if one part of the communication channel goes down, the network does not fail.

# Designing Materials for an Evolved Web

Taking the five principles of the web calls for a different approach to education and training, and a different approach to our systems and our content architecture. Our systems that currently manage and organize learning content merely create packages of digital black boxes. This means content that sits on a server or learning management system is virtually unknown to its host environment other than what a packaging standard tells it—for example, a packaging standard like the Sharable Content Object Reference Model (SCORM).

The SCORM standard requires that webpages in a course are built into modules, which are built into courses. For SCORM to work, every module needs to be identified in a manifest file along with information about how a system should track progress through the module. Is there a score to record? Is there a navigation pattern to enforce? SCORM dictates the programming code you can use to send messages to a learning management system to help ease the pain of integrating courses into systems.

Our systems are built to read the wrapping around the box, but have no sense of what may be in the box itself. Designing learning materials that are consistent with the web means designing materials that are self-aware, contextually aware, and discoverable through machine processing. To enable this, we need to create semantic structures that define our content, define the context for our content, define the different relationships our content has with other content, and create multiple ways of treating content based on our semantic structures.

This process and technology is similar in some ways to what is commonly understood as tagging, but it is also different from tagging because it is relational. Tagging is a process for wrapping content that is already written, and exposing that wrapper to machine processing. Defining semantic structures happens prior to the creation of any content and isn't meant to wrap content, but rather define it and define the relationships between various pieces of content. With tagging, there is only one relationship defined, which is all tags of the same kind go together. In semantic structures, content can be sequenced, parsed, normalized, and everything in between. Simply put, a semantic structure creates a network of relationships between various content pieces.

A quick example to showcase the difference: The tools that most instructional designers are familiar with are those that we classify as rapid development tools. Rapid development tools allow a designer to enter content into templates and publish their content into a specific format. The resulting package is then loaded onto a server (a learning management system or otherwise) where the package can be identified and even tagged by attributes like who wrote the content, what is the title of the package, a brief description, key words, and so on. The content of the course is essentially treated as a single mass of material defined by its wrapper.

A standard like DITA, which is an open source XML standard for technical documentation, not only allows you to wrap a package like a rapid development tool does but also provides a way where content inside the package is defined as being a concept, task, reference, challenge, assessment, and so on. (XML means "extensible markup language," which is a flexible way to create common information formats and share both the format and the data on the web, intranets, and elsewhere. XML describes what content is, as opposed to describing how content or data looks.) Using DITA in the content design process results in content that is searchable by a computer program by its association to concepts, or steps within tasks. A computer program could know that all steps are related to a parent structure called tasks and that all tasks had steps. This allows single words or paragraphs to be understood by computer programs.

In the example where designers are using rapid development tools, they prevent web applications from understanding the content inside a package. In the DITA example, web applications can begin to understand relationships between pieces of content and what content actually is. Exposing content to the web in the way DITA does is consistent with our five principles. It is ultimately going to fall onto the instructional designer to become familiar with building semantic structures to remain relevant as the web and people evolve, as shown in Figure 2-2.

In Figure 2-2, the products of a food store are broken down according to the various departments where they sit and to the variable characteristics that help us identify them. This model can be used to help codify products that ultimately help us locate the product if required. On the basis of the model, products will either be part of the fresh or the packaged goods section. Within fresh goods, the store has bakery, dairy, and meat items. Within dairy items, the store carries yogurt, milk, and butter. And every yogurt product in the store has the following characteristics: name, size, and price.

**Figure 2-2.** A Small Example of a Semantic Structure or Taxonomy

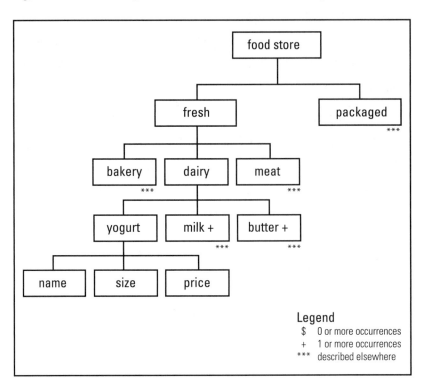

Source: Bartz, J. (2002). "Great Idea, But How Do I Do It? A Practical Example of Learning Object Creation Using SGML/XML." Canadian Journal of Learning and Technology, vol. 28 (3). Reprinted with permission.

In the next chapter, we will take a close look at the technologies that are fueling the web's continuing growth.

# Chapter 3

## New Technologies for Learning on Demand

———————● **In this chapter, you'll learn about** ●———————

- The new tools and technologies that can be leveraged for learning
  on demand
- How specific tools, like aggregating content, can make learning
  on demand more efficient and effective
- How these new tools and technologies can be used together to build
  a better platform for learning on demand

---

In chapter 2, we examined how the World Wide Web's evolution has fueled
its growth and sustains its presence. In this chapter, we explore how emerging tools and technologies that are consistent with the web's evolution will
influence the design of learning-on-demand systems.

Instructional design used to be wholly focused on taking existing content
or developing new content and shaping it into a unique event designed to
create learning. Now, however, new and emerging technologies are changing the approach to design for learning on demand, both by leveraging existing access to content and also by modeling content based on the reality that
learning can happen anywhere and anytime. These technologies include

- aggregating and curating content
- semantic searches

- predictive analytics

- natural language processing

- web analytics

- distributed networks

- remote content repositories.

This chapter introduces and explores these technologies, all of which have merit on their own and also can be used in conjunction with other technologies. Moreover, the technologies discussed in this chapter will nourish one another, support one another, and ultimately together—as opposed to working with them in pieces—provide a stronger platform on which to design learning on demand as a whole. After this chapter's introduction to these technologies, chapter 4 offers a specific vision for how they can be used collaboratively to deliver a single platform for learning on demand. First, however, it's useful to highlight some of the underlying concepts that influence these technologies' current development.

In the book *Knowledge Management in Theory and Practice*, Kimiz Dalkir (2005) describes e-learning as the capturing of "organizational memory," an essential concept for knowledge management. In creating learning products, training and development practitioners are capturing the skills and knowledge required of their employees to perform their jobs at a given moment in time and are documenting these requirements for others to use.

An important concept related to organizational memory is the distributed network, a system of interdependent units interacting to achieve one or more goals. As learning practitioners develop training programs and capture organizational memory, they capture knowledge and skills as they apply to the business rather than to individuals. Yet at any point in time, an organization possesses a collective pool of knowledge about its entire operations, and every individual contributes to this pool.

When employees are trained on an organization's inner workings, they are being given a snapshot of how the organization works and how they need to participate for it to succeed as a whole. In other words, training is not about the individual per se; it is about the system in which the individual is operating and about safeguarding the system's operation.

As the organization grows and adapts, the collective pool of knowledge is also growing and adapting, and the organization is documenting these adaptations in its training materials. Organizations engage in training to launch new products, new processes, new infrastructure, and the like. As these things change, the artifacts representing the organizational memory at a given point also need to change. It would be hard to imagine a training program that was not in some sense a subset of the collective pool of knowledge within an organization.

If e-learning is one way of representing organizational memory (Dalkir, 2005), then an e-learning course whose contents are fixed in time becomes detached from the organization's evolution. As such, the e-learning course risks harming the organization over time as it becomes less relevant to how the organization operates. It no longer trains the individual to work within the current system, but rather trains them to do something the way it used to be done.

Enter *rapid development*, the term for the tools that facilitate the design and development of e-learning in a condensed timeframe. These tools, placed in the hands of an instructional designer, produce one-person development teams capable of moving an e-learning project from start to finish. Rapid development has flourished—arising from the need to quickly design, develop, and update content—and it thus has reduced the cost of developing training programs and has enabled the quick production of learning deliverables. For instance, given the low cost of course development, it becomes easy to integrate changes in a course's content into its future iteration.

However, there is a general acceptance by the e-learning community that rapid development sacrifices some quality in the end product, and whether you buy into the practice of rapid development depends on whether you believe this sacrifice is worth it. In *Michael Allen's 2012 E-Learning Annual*, I published a chapter calling for an end to the rapid development of e-learning (Tozman, 2012). Yet my argument wasn't based on whether rapid development is worth the loss of quality but on the fact that rapid development services an archaic model of education.

Whether good or bad, rapid development tools only create individual courses for an event-driven training world. And these tools package the contents of an e-learning course into a self-contained unit. That is, other than the learning management system (LMS) that communicates with the packaging of the content (not the content itself), no other system can access the content for use outside the LMS. Taking a course built with rapid development tools and putting it on an LMS only services a model of learning where there is a teacher (the e-learning course) and a student (the learner).

It's not only rapid development tools that service a model of delivering learning as an event. Most e-learning and blended learning programs developed with tools and technologies outside rapid development also service the event-driven model. The rapid development process, however, acknowledges that content delivered as an event will probably change and is probably not worth the time and investment to create something other than that.

The event-driven learning model runs contrary to what can be called the will of the web as it evolves. Building content as an event using either rapid or other development tools will fail an organization because it is less and less relevant to how organizations are operating and structuring other facets of their operations. As the accumulation of content increases and the pace at which content changes accelerates, the attempts to create multiple content artifacts drown the organization's efficiency.

I have witnessed this firsthand when content that had been created using rapid development tools created a nightmare when it required updating. The content has been used in so many discrete boxes that it becomes a liability for an organization to try to find every instance of a particular piece of content.

For instance, in working with a large Canadian bank's training department, the volume of materials becomes so overwhelming that somebody may spend weeks trying to find where a piece of content is in the various training materials, which include e-learning, print, source files, and trainer guides. And because this financial organization is heavily regulated, it is important to be able to find any place where a policy exists that an employee might have read and acknowledged having done so. But the bank currently has no way to trace such content or find these training materials. There may be several e-learning courses, all with the same content, but nobody would know. This dire situation sets the stage for the story of how innovative web technologies can rescue us and provide a new, highly coordinated learning model, and this is what we explore in the rest of this chapter.

# Content Aggregation and Curation

For anybody who uses the web day in and day out, there is no surprise that the rate in which the web is growing vis-à-vis content is beyond what we would have imagined and possibly what we can still imagine (*The Economist,* 2010a):

- "A study in 2004 suggested that in epidemiology alone it would take *21 hours of a workday just to stay current.*"

- "When the Sloan Digital Sky Survey started work in 2000, its telescope in New Mexico collected more data in its first few weeks than had been amassed in the entire history of astronomy."

- "And whereas doctors a century ago were expected to keep up with the entire field of medicine, now they would need to be familiar with about *10,000 diseases, 3,000 drugs,* and more than *1,000 lab tests.*"

These statistics are only showing an even steeper incline as time goes on. Going back to the question of whether the web is simply a chaotic mess or a beautifully patterned vista of chaotic pockets, if we were to focus solely on the rate at which the web is expanding in content, we would be tempted to declare the web a chaotic mess. If web applications understood the content on the web, then they would be able to bring order to that chaos. As a web of pure chaos, web applications would fail. What makes the web more usable are technologies that help gather, aggregate, and curate content. Content aggregation and curation technologies help you sort through the mess and quickly find what you need.

In early web 2.0 history, services labeled *mashups* began. *Mashups* are webpages or web applications that draw in content or data from multiple external sources to create a new source of content or data. Mashups are important not only because they aggregate content from multiple sources but also because of how they do it. For example, "the Nintendo Wii has been difficult to find in stores. A web mashup might help by taking the data from various stores like EB Games and other websites like eBay and combine this information with Google maps to present you with an easy-to-use interface for finding a Wii in your area" (Daniel 2012). To draw content into a new service, mashups combine and use application programming interfaces (APIs) (see the sidebar).

## What Is an API?

APIs are widely used special handshakes between computer programs and applications. APIs are a set of rules about how to share data, content, and functional elements within an application, and the method for exchanging that information with other applications. APIs can extend one computer program's functionality by talking with other computer programs and making the data and functionality from other programs seem as if they are part of the first program. For example, when you post a message to Twitter and also have that message appear in your LinkedIn or Facebook profile, Twitter is speaking with the other sites through APIs.

In other words, mashups aren't about totally new information; they use existing content. Today, mashups are about creating an interface with other sources of information—often competing sources—to provide a user with different views of data. The importance of using APIs to draw in content from external applications or systems is a critical aspect of future learning systems that is covered in the next chapter. Although APIs don't necessarily make content or data intelligible to the web, as do tagging or metadata, they do act to strengthen a network by allowing two applications to form a distributed network where the combination of applications is stronger than either individual application.

Content aggregation makes this first pass at organizing the chaotic mess of content by grouping topics, news, authors, products, services, and so on—something like a filing cabinet. But the technology does it in real time. Doing this in real time is the actual creation of categories where no defined categories of things ever existed previous to the application running. A great example of this technology is Intel's Infoscape launched at the 2010 Computer Electronics Show (CES) in Las Vegas. The Infoscape encouraged multiple people to search the web by touching content categories represented as virtual 'panels' on a large multidimensional touchscreen surface. Each category represented topics generated from aggregated search results (Google is an aggregated search engine) coming from searches being performed at the CES conference. Every category, every panel, was an "aggregated result." Of interest was the ability to generate dozens of boxes at once when legions of onlookers decided to touch boxes simultaneously. The ability to aggregate effectively is not only dependent on the web being able to locate information, but given the pool of information it is drawing from, processing speed is critical. Intel has been working to create smaller, better, and faster chips, and its results cannot be overlooked. Although this book isn't focused on hardware improvements, when we discuss aggregation, there must be efficiency in aggregation—otherwise the technology would fade away. This is all about accessing information on demand, and if it took too long to pull in information, the on-demand aspect would be lost. Some statistics to consider:

- The number of websites as of December 2010: 255 million.

- The number of websites added in 2010: 21.4 million.

- The average Google query response time: roughly one-fourth of a second.

- The average blink of an eye: roughly one-tenth of a second.

The notion of being able to aggregate content is critical for making sense of the web—and of course for web-based learning, as we will see below and in later chapters in detail. As discussed in chapter 2, the organization of content into file folder-like paradigms is just too unruly for the pace and vastness of content on the web. The approach to content aggregation that we are interested in is one based on content relationships, whereby content is pulled into a context based on its relationship to that context. For example, think of your own email. Emails are sent by people, have subjects associated with them, and have the dates of when they were sent and received. If you use email folders, you know that it's often difficult to place an email in a specific folder because it can often belong in multiple folders. Most email software programs offer us "filtering" functionality, whereby one can sort all emails that were received on a particular date or all emails that relate to a specific subject. In this case, email content is being pulled in based on its relationship to the context of date or subject.

Here, it is necessary to expand on the concept of *context*. *Context* refers to the relevant environment that we use to understand content. Any piece of content can often be relevant to multiple people for many different reasons.

The combination of reasons why something is relevant is its *context*. And this means that context can be important in a number of ways, as noted throughout this book:

- Context helps us understand relationships between pieces of content.

- Context helps us understand the origins and intent of content.

- Context helps dictate to a learner what content he or she needs.

Thus, when I refer to context, I generally mean those factors that make two disparate pieces of content relate to one another, through one or more environmental factors, such as:

- For whom is the content relevant?

- What is the content subject matter?

- Who created the content?

In this way, content has multiple access points and can be retrieved on demand in a multitude of ways. A great example of this technology, and one that has been around for a while, is the Visual Thesaurus see (Figure 3-1) (www.visualthesaurus.com).

The Visual Thesaurus web application seen in Figure 3-1 is searching for content based on a user's search, processing the user's request, and exposing a series of relationships based on this request. In this example, the *context* is the term for which the user is searching. The returned result shows that any single term—which is our context—may have multiple relationships. The program builds out the map of relationships based on the term chosen by the

**Figure 3-1.** The Visual Thesaurus Website

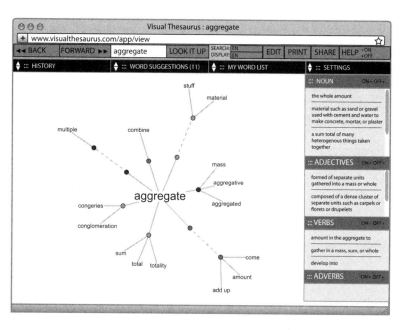

user (the word they look up). The key is that any term searched or any term retrieved may have multiple relationships with other terms. Think about the documents in your computer today. Most likely they are in a single folder, but they could well be in multiple folders. Aggregation technology that uses relationships doesn't classify items based on category. It aggregates a particular piece of content based on its relationship with other pieces of content. Aggregation technology based on relationships will prevail because it is the technology that is most consistent with the will of the web outlined in this book.

# Semantic Searches

Before exploring the meaning of semantic web searches, it's important to acknowledge the power that web searches in general have given us—the power to find information and ultimately serve up great potential for learning. The role of the ability to search cannot be understated in the vision of a learning-on-demand system. Not only is searching for information an act to begin the process of learning on demand; it is also a way to expose ourselves to the web. Web analytics is being used almost everywhere—tracking what we search for, when we search for it, and what results we acknowledge. By tracking this information, applications learn what our interests are and can feed this information to other applications and systems.

All search engines, whether semantic or not, are constantly indexing content on the web, regardless of whether anybody is searching or not. This process is done through *web crawlers*, which are little pieces of programming that are constantly scanning webpages and bringing back results to be stored and then accessed during searches. This is how search engines are able to seemingly execute a new search and bring back results in fractions of a second.

A semantic search looks much like what we are all used to, which for lack of a better way to explain it, is a Google search. But a semantic search has key differences from a regular search, which stem from the principle that a semantic search tries to understand the *meaning* of your search.

Remember our hockey analogy in the introduction, and the task of using Google to find an offensive defenseman? Google doesn't know that we are trying to limit our searches for defenseman. Google will try to match the combination of words together, but will also retrieve results based on the individual terms. So if I search for "offensive defenseman," my search results will yield results that include offensive players in addition to defensive players.

Running semantic searches on the content of the web today will only show minimal improvement over the relevancy of results from traditional search engines. This is because content that sits on the web hasn't yet been normalized—that is, we don't yet have a consistent way of drawing relationships between the various pieces of content. Aside from the business of returning results, semantic search engines go about the business of crawling the web and indexing pieces of content differently.

The relevance of a semantic search is tied directly to both the goal of having web applications understand content and the prospect of personalizing your web experience. Matching words on a page with words in a search bar is different than being able to automatically index content. A web application's ability to search through a webpage and—without any presence of tagging— know that a word may be the name of a city, is the ability to understand content versus simply reading it.

At a user conference, I was privy to seeing a "tagging engine" scour through a webpage and find names, addresses, geographic locations, and more. The most impressive thing was its accuracy. Consider what is currently a default functionality on our smartphones. If someone sends us an email with a telephone number in the message, our phones are able to detect it in context and create a link to dial the number automatically. This is a great example of a web application automatically understanding content within the web. It is important to note that in this example, the web is simply guessing what a phone number is because there is nothing about the content that says "I am a name" or "I am a telephone number."

As for the personalization aspect to a semantic search, while the search is trying to understand the meaning of what you want, it is also trying to render back personalized results. The search is not only matching words that would be the same for everybody; it is also doing its best to understand *your* intentions. Early experiments with semantic search engines entailed constantly gathering analytics about what you were looking for and then being able to apply those patterns to your searches with more and more accuracy to what you would look for in the future.

Although we've briefly discussed the difference between semantic searches and today's common search engines, it is worthwhile to dive in a little deeper. Whereas today's search engines rely on tags and external information, semantic search engines are trying to understand what's on the page. A benefit of this kind of search is that the results returned do not simply consist of a link to a webpage, where the searcher will still need to take steps to find the information they need; rather, the results brought back include the content itself that relates to the search. Visually, this may be the actual content appearing in the results page with key terms highlighted. As an example, try your own search on Hakia, which has been called the "first meaning-based search engine" (see www.hakia.com).

To the degree that a semantic search engine tries to understand the meaning of content on a page, it is also trying to understand the search itself that we have mentioned. We look at *natural reasoning engines* in this chapter within their own right, but it's important to discuss them here in the context of a semantic search as well. As these engines apply to a semantic search, they are called *natural language queries* and refer to a machine's ability to understand the intent of the search. Again, using Hakia's description, here is their take on this:

A semantic search engine is expected to respond sensibly when the query is in a question form (what, where, how, why, and so on). Note that a "search engine" is different than a "question-answering" system. Search engine's main task is to rank search results in the most logical and relevant manner whereas a question-answering system may produce a single extracted entity. The example query "How fast is swine flu spreading?" brings a result set in Hakia to shed light to this capability (Hakia, 2011).

Thus, Hakia sets out to find the answer to your searches, not necessarily trying to bring in pages that match the words in your search.

# Predictive Analytics

While this book was being written, IBM (2011) released the story "New IBM Software Helps Analyze the World's Data for Healthcare Transformation," which describes a new technology that is able to crawl through content and provide healthcare practitioners with relevant information at the time of need about patient care. This technology uses what is known as *predictive analytics* to not only scour through the past and present, but also to predict the future. Thus, by letting a doctor find out more about individual patients, predictive analytics will enable healthcare organizations to better analyze patients' needs and avoid releasing patients too soon.

Predictive analytics encompasses a variety of statistical techniques—modeling, machine learning, data mining, and game theory—that analyze current and historical facts to make predictions about future events (Wikipedia, 2011). Its first application will be to help healthcare providers improve on readmission practices for their patients by looking at the root causes of re-admissions. Thus, IBM's solution will scour through data, develop trends for data using analytics, and provide insight where it was previously unavailable. The truly astonishing aspect of this technology is its ability to scour through unstructured data, as opposed to structured data—see the sidebar for the difference between these two types of data.

## Structured Versus Unstructured Data

What is the difference between structured and unstructured data? According to Search Storage (2007b), structured data are "really data... organized in a structure so that it is identifiable. The most universal form of structured data is a database like SQL or Access [that]...allows you to select specific pieces of information based on columns and rows in a field." Conversely, unstructured data have "no identifiable structure. Unstructured data typically includes...data types that are not part of a database. Most enterprise data today can actually be considered unstructured. An email is considered unstructured data. Even though the email messages themselves are organized in a database... the body of the message is really freeform text without any structure at all—the data is considered raw."

Structured data are identifiable by machines. They are data that are designated as part of a group. For example, consider a table in a database called "address" and a row in the table called "zip code." A computer can understand a value entered into zip code (following proper formatting), in addition to being part of a larger group called address.

Unstructured data cannot be identified by machines; text, images, and tables on a webpage are unstructured. According to Search Storage (2007a):

---

A big part of the problem is identifying the unstructured data in order to manage it. For example, if you're looking at bitmap images, seismic data, audio or video, there is no way to really identify the data other than the filename and extension—there is no way to "look" at the data and know that a given piece of data comprises an image or other data type. This makes essential management tasks—like data identification, classification, legal discovery, and even basic searches—very challenging for the enterprise.

---

Scouring through structured data isn't something new, and it is the ideal state for machines, because the notion of structure implies a format that can be understood by a machine. Thus far, the volume of unstructured data far outweighs structured data; and therefore contained in this data is a wealth of valuable information that cannot be quickly consumed and parsed. But the new technology for predictive analytics bridges this gap. It is an engine for unstructured data that can make sense of it and therefore compute it.

# Natural Language Processing

Imagine the power of a search engine that could distinguish between these two statements:

1. Jane saw a plane flying over Zurich.

2. Jane saw a mountain flying over Zurich.

Imagine what your "search" tool provider can do for you when it understands the nuance in language. These search engines are *natural language reasoning engines*. They understand the nuance in language, thus making queries more effective.

An example of a natural language reasoning engine is OpenCyc, an experimental database containing innumerable statements of fact. In addition to being a database of facts, it also has a natural language reasoning engine that allows OpenCyc to *compute*, based on the statements already contained in the database. This may seem slightly obtuse, but the results of OpenCyc are very impressive. OpenCyc is able to distinguish statements, such as the two statements given above, so it knows that in statement 1, Jane was on the ground watching a plane fly above, and that in statement 2, she was in a plane viewing a mountain below.

# Web Analytics

A 2010 *Economist* article "The Data Deluge" describes the issue of data volume that is being amassed by business intelligence analytics, web analytics, and other analytic engines. The volume of data that now exists creates a real issue for those responsible for trying to make sense of it. Figuring out what is and isn't meaningful becomes overwhelming when so much data is coming in (*The Economist*, 2010b). Analytic engines not only gather data; they also provide dashboard views of the data to help the interpretation of that data. The largest issue facing analytic companies is how to format the dashboard view of data. What view delivers the stories that are significant within the data?

Thus far, our focus in this chapter has been to showcase key technology trends that will have an impact on the future of learning and the systems used to manage learning materials and learning activities. The field of analytics for business intelligence, and particularly web analytics for our purposes, has matured and grown considerably and showcases impressive engines for trending data. At the same time, analytics for education for the most part has remained antiquated and irrelevant. Traditional learning management systems focus on binary measurements of outcomes—for example; complete versus incomplete, or passed versus failed.

We have always assumed that learning happens during instruction. Another way to look at learning is as a response to instruction. Where instruction is a *stimulus*, learning is a *response*. If we assume that learning happens during instruction, then we are also saying that the learning is contained within the instruction and thus there is a one-to-one relationship between instruction and learning. We have always designed this way.

Imagine delivering instruction where the objective is to change behavior A. After delivering the instruction, you find that the audience has instead changed behavior B. Has the instruction failed? Has the audience not "learned"? We all enter the same experience carrying different baggage and perspectives, so would it be unusual for different people to learn different things from the same experience?

Collecting a binary analytic of passed versus not passed as a reflection of learning works—if what you create is a one-to-one relationship between instruction and learning. A case can be made that it would be difficult to find any reliable measurement of learning when the individual's expression of having learned something may or may not conform to what you believe that expression should be. What I would like to propose is having a look at modern-day web analytics or business intelligence analytics that show real potential for collecting data on *value*.

Web analytic engines help measure and trend traffic to and from websites. The technology and the vision for web analytics apply directly to what training and learning professionals do. Learning professionals need to understand and embrace this technology. To provide you with an accurate portrait of web analytics and where that field is heading, I interviewed a sales engineer from a large analytics company that services large media corporations and content providers. He summed up the situation this way:

---

Web analytics measures experience to change outcomes. Right now, the greatest challenge for analytics is the overload of data and gleaning actionable insights is tough. The holy grail for companies is in the data. . . . Companies are investing in data collection, but they minimize what we provide when they talk about it as "metrics." "Metrics" are not the business objectives for most organizations that are investing. Essentially, analytics gives us the digital world in a database. How it's used is different for different businesses…

---

Imagine a large media company that provides online content. Its main business objective is to increase visits and consumption of its content so the company can sell more advertising. What it wants to glean from the data are things like: Who are my referrers? Which referrer creates the most clicks per visit? Identifying referrers that create multiple clicks per visit provides insight on how you may be able to increase overall traffic to the site.

With the rise of social media and the ability to track device use, we are now able to stitch together profiles. Because of the convergence of profiles such as Facebook and Twitter, we are able to glean things about people's profiles from Facebook and see what they talk about in Twitter. We're able to build profiles of habits and therefore help companies target more effectively. Companies are able to provide dynamically built pages against profiles of people. Eventually they will be able to do this at an individual level.

Right now, we're exploring multichannel analytics and predictive analytics. Predictive analytics is all about building relationships from the other. For systems where individuals authenticate in a system, it's easier to build profiles. But when individuals don't, we're using predictive analytics to draw out individual profiles from the cloud of data. At another company I worked at, we used *panel data*, which is the installation of software on a sample of our end user's machines that collected data about their use of the computer. I found that the results it brought back were not very reliable. So the use of predictive analytics tries to do the same thing.

The clients of analytics are the businesses themselves. If they choose to translate the analytics to service their clients, then that is their objective. So whereas analytics in and of itself doesn't necessarily feed into the principle of learning on demand, it does service many aspects of a learning business.

# Distributed Networks

In his book *The Learning Layer*, Steven Flinn (2010) presents the case for enabling machines to provide a layer within a business that facilitates employee performance on the job. The learning layer provides employees with access to tacit and explicit knowledge within an organization and is constantly evolving through its own learning. To understand the structure of a learning layer, it's important to understand the idea of a distributed network.

We mentioned distributed networks above, and another way to understand them is to look at the evolution of artificial intelligence and the field of robotics. The first robots were built to have a single brain that controlled everything. The robot was modeled after our own concept of how our brains work. But what the robotics engineers discovered is that there is far too much complexity involved in building a single brain that controls everything. Conversely, robots with limited functionality and smaller sets of programming logic did very well.

So the robotic community moved to a *distributed network of brains*, whereby a single robot had a network of smaller brains, each with its own limited set of operations, including communication protocols with the other brains with which it needed to interact. Think about a robot whose appendages had a brain, its internal subsystems had a brain, its head a brain, and so on—more brains, fewer faculties and functions within each brain. Each brain has fewer lines of logic code that is responsible for how the controlled area behaves under what conditions, what to do with inputs from other areas, and what outputs are required to other areas.

In a distributed network, there are many control centers, each of which is self-sufficient. The sum of all control centers is greater than the simple addition of all centers one by one. In other words, 1 + 1 = 3.

As this applies to analytics and *the learning layer*, there isn't one machine collecting and reporting data. There is a distributed network; there is a system that is monitoring and reporting back usage and users; and, most important, the system itself is learning as it continually interacts.

It is this concept of "learning as it interacts" that is critical. Flinn talks of a "fuzzy network" when he describes how a network learns. Similar to the distributed network, a fuzzy network contains not only relationships but also analytics such as *weights* around objects and relationships. The addition of analytics to a relationship is what allows a network to learn. It's what allows a network to evolve, since without the constant stream of analytics, the relationships remain stagnant. If you are a subscriber to Netflix, then you know about the email you receive after viewing a movie that asks you to rate the movie. Your rating of the movie is a *weight* that gets associated with it. In addition to your weighting of it, there is also your profile that is associated with your feedback. As more people weight the film, the more the Netflix system understands what kinds of profiles prefer what kinds of movies. The Netflix system is learning to whom to recommend which movies. And this can likewise be applied in the context of learning on demand. For example, imagine that you went searching for content to help you learn about a particular topic and found multiple resources that might help. As you went through these resources, you could indicate whether they were helpful or not. Now imagine that several people later perform this same search, and each one of them indicates whether a resource was helpful or not. Still later, if you were to again perform this same search, you would now be able to see patterns of what was helpful to people and what wasn't.

# Using Analytics to Help Machines Learn

Essentially, the *learning layer* is a great example of using analytics to help machines learn. For the most part, analytics has been used to help tell a story—and sometimes many substories. For instance, when Amazon began to recommend reading to its customers based on their purchases, it was using the analytics within its system. Amazon has records of everything its customers buy and what a customer buys together in a single purchase.

Even more powerful are Amazon's stored profiles, which keep historical data not only on what is purchased together at one time but also on someone's entire purchasing history. Over time, some patterns emerge that are stronger than others, and machines can effectively begin to predict behavior based on the same statistical formulas we use to predict things like "death by heart attack every year" and "death by heart attack in the United States every year versus Canada." In other words, Amazon's recommendations become increasingly prescriptive the more data it has to predict your shopping habits.

A content provider's ability to offer its consumers dynamically built web-pages based on their user profiles is a great example of how machines can learn through analytics and is a great way to understand the learning layer. For example, in the context of learning on demand, the managers of an organization's professional development program can develop curricula using the organization's intranet on demand and in real time. And one of this program's features is that it gathers data on what the managers are bundling together for the curriculum.

Let's look at a similar example from an uncommon but very interesting and poetically appropriate workplace: the world's largest physical library, the Library of Congress. A single facilitator running a professional development workshop may decide to use the library's curriculum materials for analyzing photographs (a subject with an activity stream—which is a list of recent activities performed by an individual, typically on a single website—defined by the library's curriculum designers). For example, within the subject area "Analyzing Photographs," there are three to four activities that a facilitator may want to include in a session. The library's website accommodates a facilitator who wants to take an activity used in another subject area with multiple activity streams, "Analyzing Music," and bundle it with the "Analyzing Photographs" activities. What if the majority of facilitators do the same thing? In the library's system, the data about which activities are being bundled together are captured and then brought back to the facilitators as they pick and choose activities to help them know what others have found helpful. And as the system accrues more and more users, it is able to generate recommendations that are increasingly valuable.

To some degree, machines' ability to learn from analytics answers questions about how learners will acquire knowledge in a self-directed way when they don't know what they don't know. Using analytics is part of a solution that facilitates self-directed learning—because analytics has the power of history behind it.

Analytics doesn't only help match people to content based on their profiles; it also matches people to content when they don't fit the profile. In my analytics interview quoted earlier in the chapter, the interviewee talked about stitching profiles together based on a person's web browsing patterns. Because machines are empowered through profiles, machines will also learn when profiles don't fit an individual. And machines will then begin to build new profiles based on individuals who seemingly were part of a pattern but then deviated.

Picture a 25-year-old female using her iPad in the evening, looking at CNN's news on the Middle East. The system has captured this profile, and it begins to provide dynamically assembled content based on what other 25-year-old females browsing Middle Eastern politics on CNN via an iPad have seen. The current 25-year-old female returns to the home page upon seeing the system-generated content because none of it interested her, and she goes to sports news instead. The system checks to see if there are any profiles with similar browsing patterns or other profiles that have a close match. So now the system has captured data on the discrete pieces of content that have been viewed and the navigation patterns in which the content has been viewed.

## Remote Content Repositories

One of the requirements that existing learning management systems are beginning to change is the need for all content to reside locally on the same machine as the learning management system software itself. All the courses that are in your LMSs are probably all sitting on the same computer box as the LMS software. The committees that design standards for how content management systems (CMSs) and LMSs interact have begun to deploy standards that allow content to sit outside an LMS and still have the LMS launch the course as though it were sitting locally and tracking student progress. This change will help avoid duplication of content and will allow changes to content to happen outside the LMS without having to again upload courses into the LMS. This change is leading to the development of what are called remote content repositories (RCRs). But to explain RCRs, it's best to first look at CMSs and whom they service.

## The Difference Between a CMS and an LMS

Though they are often confused, there are distinct differences between a CMS and a LMS. Most important, a CMS faces the nonlearner and an LMS faces the learner. A CMS is where content is stored, assembled, and managed. A LMS is where content is delivered to the student and the student experiences it being managed.

A CMS stores discrete pieces of content (audio, video, text, flash, PDFs, documents, and so on) so that they may be assembled in a variety of ways while maintaining a single version of the content. The business problem that the CMS solves is having multiple versions of the same file scattered through an organization and the difficulty in retrieving the latest version so that it can be used elsewhere. Most CMSs offer a variety of version control systems (to maintain and index a file as it is modified throughout its history) and workflow systems (which give permissions for content stakeholders to use the content and edit it). First-generation CMSs—for example, IBM's Content Manager and OpenText—and most learning CMSs required a content administrator to assemble content, package it, and then export it from the CMS and move the package to its destination (a LMS, in our world). CMS technology did evolve so that it can work through APIs, with other systems eliminating the need to bring content out and then back in to another application.

Now we again arrive at the RCR, which is a storage area for content that sits between the interface that a learner or content consumer uses (the LMS) and the source content sitting in the CMS. The content within the RCR can be manipulated through the consumer interface, the LMS. The RCR allows this content to be manipulated by the consumer yet controlled by the content administrator. The other purpose of the RCR is to create multiple access points or interfaces. To make this feasible, APIs (again, special handshakes between computer programs and applications) are developed to enable other applications to access and manipulate the content.

How does the content consumer manipulate content? One of the most relevant ways is by aggregating the content into personalized packages. If you think about the LMS model, every training course has a set table of contents, which is made up of independent learning objects. An online course has been packaged in a specific format (for example, HTML, Flash, or HTML5) and thus has preselected modules ready for you. And in a world where content no longer sits in an LMS but sits in an RCR, the learner can choose not only his or her own skill modules but also the package's format. As for the content administrator, he or she is pushing content into the RCR from the CMS by telling the RCR what the content they are pushing into it is, as well as the formats that the content can support.

The best way to think about an RCR is in terms of its closest business model, the off-the-shelf library of online content that an organization may acquire for its employees. These off-the-shelf content libraries cover a range of soft skills and technical skills, like using Microsoft Word. However, the big difference between content libraries and RCRs is that libraries only offer users the finished product of the content. The library provides access to a course, a curriculum, or a series of both. But an RCR provides a gateway to the pool of raw content, allowing the consumer to create their own products from this pool. How would this actually function? Consider Figure 3-2 and the sidebar.

**Figure 3-2.** How a Remote Content Repository Functions

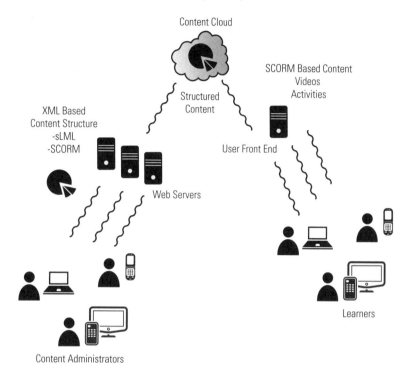

## Cloud Technology

Cloud technology, which is a proliferating part of the world of RCRs, is driving innovation and change in systems design. In the most general sense, *the cloud* is the Internet. It represents everything that lives in the ethereal body known as the web. *Cloud-based services* are run from a hosted supplier, and thus there is no local installation of the services that the consumer uses on her computer. The use of the word *service* points to why someone would use the hosted application. For example, GoogleDocs provides a cloud-based word-processing service.

## How RCRs Work

Technologically, the business process for an RCR begins with an external web application accessing the content within an RCR. Upon accessing the RCR, the external application identifies itself to the RCR ("I am Bank of Canada") and sends it a host of other requirements (such as a device business unit). Using APIs, the application passes this information to the RCR, and the RCR responds by allowing the web application to access the content that is appropriate for the context sent to it by the web application. The RCR's effectiveness is based on content that the learning-on-demand web application can understand. In the learning-on-demand system, the RCR is an intelligent content delivery system servicing multiple clients with multiple needs in a single location.

However, when we refer to *cloud technology*, something much more specific is meant—usually, the information technology configuration of an environment based on virtualization. *Virtualization* is the ability to create a virtual instance of a software application frozen in time, and thus to deploy software without needing to install it anywhere. Virtualization replicates an instance of software as an image, which can be manipulated as though it were the real thing. For example, desktop virtualization has been around for quite some time, as have business models that use application service providers (ASPs). ASPs are very similar to today's software-as-a-service model, whereby software applications are hosted by a vendor as opposed to installed directly on a machine. So what is the difference between ASPs and cloud technology?

To answer this question, let's first consider this conversational snippet from a software supplier who moved his software to the cloud: "So a single client can basically launch three portals with different URLs and different looks—but all running from the same LMS." The fact that the supplier can launch three different portals, with different URLs and different looks, in minutes, shows how cloud technology differs from ASPs. With ASPs, a consumer had access to a software platform the way that the supplier conceived and made it. But with cloud technology, the supplier can use virtualization and APIs to deliver variations of his software in minutes.

The application of cloud technology is revolutionizing the business models for how suppliers provide their services, as well as leading to a convergence of technologies into a technology mashup. Thus, it is possible to construct a new piece of software by integrating various cloud-based services into a new model whose newness is simply the amalgamation of existing technologies (remember the mashup?).

Although cloud-based services are extremely important for the technologies that are contributing to the web's new design imperatives, they are beyond the scope of this book. For our purposes, it is sufficient to grasp the notion of software that can be rendered differently for various users, yet all feed from the same base software installation. In this regard, it is also important to understand that the components of a cloud-based universe speak to one another through APIs, which allow different software services to understand one another, as well as allow the content within the services to be understood and usable. Thus, machines are able to seamlessly move about the cloud-based universe in their own unique ways, processing cloud-based services and information.

Figure 3-3 shows what's important about cloud technology. In the figure, a central cloud is able to spawn versions of itself in slightly different configurations. Each smaller cloud services different device requirements. In other words, the service provided by the main cloud doesn't respond the same way, regardless of the device accessing it. Its spawned clouds can accommodate the unique features of the different devices without requiring a change to the core application. Each little cloud is pulling what it needs from the master cloud. And it's all dynamic, so only the master cloud needs upkeep.

**Figure 3-3.** What's Important About Cloud Technology?

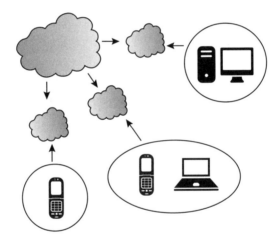

# Summing Up: New Technologies, New Design Strategies

The technologies discussed in this chapter are all contributing to a new design paradigm for instructional designers by empowering them to think creatively about how content can be deployed, not just designed. There are as many roles for instructional designers as there are aptitudes within the field. The technologies discussed above give all of us a new playground, a new set of rules, and opportunities to have an impact on our organizations.

In this chapter, again, we've looked at technologies that are consistent with the principles discussed in chapter 2:

- aggregating and curating content

- semantic searches

- predictive analytics

- natural language processing

- web analytics

- distributed networks

- remote content repositories.

As the web is continuously fed and its content grows exponentially, we need technologies that can round up the disparate pieces of content and draw links for us through common threads to make the web intelligent for applications and users. The technologies discussed in this chapter all have great potential when we discuss learning systems, especially if considered together as an ecosystem. From this perspective, semantic searches enable users to understand the meaning of the search itself, rather than simply matching words. The power of semantic searches will increase as content on the web becomes more structured, because they will be able to create relationships between pieces of content that simple word matchups would never be able to accomplish. And semantic search technology is strengthened by the presence of natural language reasoning engines, which are designed for question/

answer relationships. Not only can this technology be applied at the search level, but it can also help in returning data or content that is targeted to a user's inquiry. Semantic searches and natural language reasoning engines cater to a user base that enjoys self-directed learning. And thus they are tools that will ultimately service a learning-on-demand world.

The evolution of web analytics is important because it captures data so that we can assess our own projects and make decisions about how our learners are consuming content and applying this content in various contexts. Analytics is an essential component in helping machines learn, and it ultimately helps them understand the content and deliver more personalized learning experiences.

Remote content repositories are helping content providers offer a different model to their consumers, one that allows the consumer to choose both the content and its delivery format. This service is even further refined through the use of cloud-based technologies, whereby the web becomes a complex but efficient network of services and content—all programmed to speak with and understand each other.

If we look at the technology-based learning industry, we see *social learning* and now *content curation* that uses e-learning and talks of performance support. This industry has virtual worlds, gaming, experiential learning, and a host of very complex services. However, if we compare the emerging technologies discussed in this chapter with the current model for delivering all our complex learning products and services, we see two contrasting worlds.

In the existing world of training and development, learning content is segregated from the systems and technologies used by the rest of businesses. But in the learning-on-demand world, learning systems are integrated into the systems and technologies that are feeding the rest of businesses. As businesses wrestle with the volume of content and the lightning pace of content changes, they adopt the empowering technologies described here that more effectively collect data and deliver content. But instructional designers, by designing and developing content the way they have done until now, alienate the training and development function from these business improvements.

Those in the training and development field tend to use technology to service an old model of education. If we compare and contrast the opportunities that technology presents—where content is connected through relationships with people, where people are connected through relationships with content, and where machines learn more about us and create new connections—we are left with an impasse in relation to the existing training and development world.

Training and development's existing paradigm for innovation is about feeding content to local servers with increasing ease, integrating social media as though they were an appendage to this large static body of training, and trying to create engagement with learners through videos. Whereas the web is facilitating content on demand, training and development is continuing to service a model where experts dictate what's right and wrong. The web began to radically shift how content is consumed a long time ago, and it has now made possible an intelligent content-on-demand model. It incorporates the web learning more and more about us, to account for a 100 percent totally self-directed passage through content. With an intelligent web of content, learners have more to gain through self-directed exploration than through the existing hierarchy of teachers and learners.

Using old technologies to service an old model of education means ignoring the opportunities offered by the new technologies outlined in this chapter. The web has disrupted our ways of communicating and consuming content. Change is required, and in the next chapter we explore this change and what future learning systems will look like.

# Chapter 4

## Structuring a Learning-on-Demand System

━━━━━● **In this chapter, you'll learn about** ●━━━━━

- How to build a learning-on-demand system, using components based on emerging tools and technologies
- The relationships between these tools and technologies in supporting learning on demand
- What's different about learning on demand when accessed through these tools and technologies

---

In chapter 3, we explored emerging tools and technologies that were consistent with the five key characteristics of the web discussed in chapter 2. In this chapter, we look at those tools and technologies that are specifically designed to work with one another to create a new type of platform based on the principles of learning on demand. This chapter offers an alternative vision of what a learning system could look like and the benefits offered when the tools and technologies presented in the last chapter are intentionally designed for learning on demand.

The term *learning-on-demand system* is used in this context as a hub that supports and influences workplace learning. It interfaces with the organization as a whole, both feeding from and contributing to *organizational memory*. The learning-on-demand system described here should at the very least help us pause and reflect on our models for distributing learning content. The vision provided here is meant to be disruptive. Why? Because it turns traditional models on their heads and instead leads with the principles of learner control, intelligent processing by machines to support personal goals, and the flattening of learning organizations where learners, teachers, and subject matter experts contribute equally to the intelligence and strength of the network. For more on this creative disruption, see the sidebar.

## The Value of Creative Disruption

Sugata Mitra, the principal architect of the "Hole-in-the-Wall" experiments, tells us that this disruption is not only a viable alternative to traditional learning systems but also an efficient one. Let's look at his experiments (Hole-in-the-Wall, 2011):

*Sugata Mitra, Chief Scientist at NIIT [National Institute of Information Technology], is credited with the discovery of Hole-in-the-Wall. As early as 1982, he had been toying with the idea of unsupervised learning and computers. Finally, in 1999, he decided to test his ideas in the field. On January 26th, Dr. Mitra's team carved a "hole in the wall" that separated the NIIT premises from the adjoining slum in Kalkaji, New Delhi. Through this hole, a freely accessible computer was put up for use. This computer proved to be an instant hit among the slum dwellers, especially the children. With no prior experience, the children learned to use the computer on their own. This prompted Dr. Mitra to propose the following hypothesis: The acquisition of basic computing skills by any set of children can be achieved through incidental learning provided the learners are given access to a suitable computing facility, with entertaining and motivating content and some minimal (human) guidance.*

The results of Mitra's experiments are fascinating. In one case, an experiment was to leave a computer with a classroom of children who were given the task of learning biotechnology. After two months, Mitra was astounded to learn that children were able to teach themselves approximately 30 percent of what they would need to pass an exam on their own.

# Interest-Based Learning

We have always believed that instructional designers, teachers, and educators design content in a way that almost magically moves the learning encoded in our designs directly into the brains of our learners. We believe that we play a critical role in developing learners with the skills they need to succeed through crafting the best designs possible. What we learn from Dr. Mitra and through simple observation of people using the web is that *interest-based learning—* learning without intentional design—is incredibly effective as well.

The learning-on-demand systems discussed in this chapter are meant to support new learning models based on maximizing performance in the workplace and self-directed, interest-based learning. The learning-on-demand system will also support existing training models, where learners are asked to complete instruction that they may have no interest in taking, other than its application to their work.

In the context of natural learning habits, when we set out to learn something new, we don't necessarily know what we're going to learn. Yet as instructional designers, we have always worked to limit incidental learning by focusing content design on what we believe somebody needs to learn. But if we could instead start with natural learning habits, we'd make sure to include a childlike sense of wonder as things pop up and grab our attention. If we learn naturally by wondering, and thus letting our minds wander freely, why do instructional designers work so hard to limit that experience?

At this point, you may be thinking that the process of defining objectives and ensuring the instruction meets these objectives is all part of the reasons you control the experience. A learning-on-demand system recognizes that learning is a result of experience and not the experience itself. Limiting the experience of instruction to only the content that matches the objectives is to undermine the individual responses to the experience that people may have. Opening the experience as it relates to the objectives of instruction to relationships outside the objectives will allow individuals going through instruction to build a personal experience from what the designer has assembled.

A model of a learning-on-demand system opens up learning opportunities and encourages learners to create their own experiences. At the same time, we still need to guide the learner for maximum benefits and somewhat limit the mental wandering. The components of a learning-on-demand system enable a model where interest-based learning thrives, and the needs for any necessary controls are also met. At the same time, a learning-on-demand system is also structured to deliver prescriptive learning. The main components are:

- structured content input: administrator/user

- normalization of data

- metadata

- the analytics framework

- remote content repositories

- APIs and web services

- separating content from form and function

- content aggregators

- the roles of users

- social networking media as feedback loops and evolution

- semantic search.

The rest of this chapter explores these components in detail, and then we'll consider how the components work together.

# Structured Content Input: Administrator/User

Learning-on-demand systems thrive based on the same principles that make up the will of the web. Learners, mentors, and teachers will all feed content to the learning-on-demand system. This will help our system evolve and grow based on the strengthening of the network. Feeding a learning-on-demand system with content is essential. Much like the web itself, feeding a learning-on-demand system strengthens the network of learning resources available to consumers.

The difference between learning-on-demand systems and conventional learning systems is the spectrum of content contributors who feed the network, all of whom play an equally important role in strengthening the network. Traditionally teachers, subject matter experts, and content administrators posted "official" content to the learning system to be consumed by learners. This is very consistent with current educational models, where there are teachers and students, with teachers transmitting information and the learners receiving that information.

We can trace this model back to earlier formal education systems, where apprentices learned from masters. This is where the web has been such a disruptive force, because what was once tacit knowledge in the hands of masters is now a wealth of explicit knowledge from networks of masters and students alike, available for consumption when you need it and how you need it.

## Tacit vs. Explicit Knowledge

Tacit knowledge is knowledge hidden mostly in someone's head. Explicit knowledge is accessible through an open channel not dependent on the presence of a person.

Before the web, the single most popular place to get explicit knowledge based on self-interest was the library. When I was younger, going to the library was something special. It was a time when I could find books that I liked, spend some time looking them over, and finally choose books to take home. Browsing the web is very similar. Think of the web as the largest library of books in the world. We move from interest to interest within a single stream of experiences, except that the web isn't limited to just books. There are books, opinions, articles, images, videos, audio files, and everything in between. All these components allow us to serve our own self-interest through content presented in multiple ways, and learn from it. A learning-on-demand system is structured around the same principles of learning as a stream of fluid experiences, allowing users to decide what's valuable to them based on the aggregate pool of content.

This is a critical concept to grasp. Classes, group meetings, and study sessions are all scheduled events around a singular purpose generally defined by a group leader or teacher. Miss the event and you miss the learning. In a learning-on-demand environment, it is an environment rife with potential learning experiences controlled by the learner with no beginning and no end. So how do learners dive in? Where do they start, and where do they end?

This is where the principle of a web application that can understand content comes into play. It is equally important for learning-on-demand systems to understand the content it is being fed as it is to allow for content to be fed from a variety of contributors. A learning-on-demand system wants to know who is feeding it content, what kind of content it is, to what the content relates, and who are the ideal consumers for the content. To accomplish this goal, the system must provide an interface for contributors to create new content from scratch and add existing content (like a PDF) in a format that the system will understand.

This means the learning-on-demand environment needs an interface that allows for content structuring. "Structured" here means the normalization of data and the semantic markup of content. Remember the hockey example from the introduction? In that example, shown again here as Figure 4-1, we needed to ensure that the players' attributes were all represented in the same format.

**Figure 4-1.** The Hockey Example Redux

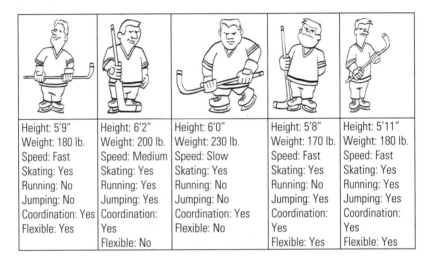

| Height: 5'9" | Height: 6'2" | Height: 6'0" | Height: 5'8" | Height: 5'11" |
|---|---|---|---|---|
| Weight: 180 lb. | Weight: 200 lb. | Weight: 230 lb. | Weight: 170 lb. | Weight: 180 lb. |
| Speed: Fast | Speed: Medium | Speed: Slow | Speed: Fast | Speed: Fast |
| Skating: Yes | Skating: Yes | Skating: Yes | Skating: Yes | Skating: Yes |
| Running: No | Running: Yes | Running: No | Running: No | Running: Yes |
| Jumping: No | Jumping: Yes | Jumping: No | Jumping: Yes | Jumping: Yes |
| Coordination: Yes | Coordination: Yes | Coordination: Yes | Coordination: Yes | Coordination: Yes |
| Flexible: Yes | Flexible: No | Flexible: No | Flexible: Yes | Flexible: Yes |

# Normalization of Data

Normalization of data refers to the standardization for how data are represented in a computer program. A simple example would be the various ways in which people enter dates—Jan. 1, 2012; 01/01/12; Jan 1, 12; and so on. Finding a consistent way to show data is called *normalization*.

Normalization will happen in two different ways depending on whether we are creating net new content or contributing existing content. The normalization process for net new content uses a form-like interface that guides somebody to enter new content into buckets and provides a range of metadata elements around the bucket. Normalization for existing content is only required if there are differences in how the same content is currently represented. For example, content that includes dates might represent those dates differently. For computer programs to understand dates, the ways in which dates get entered into the system must somehow all be the same.

## Normalizing New Content

The first type of content that we need to normalize is new content. Normalization, which we encountered in the context of the hockey players in the introduction, is built into the design process. In a learning-on-demand system, the normalization of new content needs to happen before you ever write content through an interface, which guides the normalization process throughout the creation of content. Thus, the interface for contributing new content to a learning-on-demand system has the structure and elements that dictate the relationships between the pieces of content embedded in the authoring interface.

To help understand what structuring new content might look like, consider the sLML specification. Structured Learning Markup Language (sLML) is an open source learning markup language available through sourceforge.com. The sLML specification provides a common structure for authoring content. The structure of sLML is based on five categories of common performance outcomes (or objectives) in a corporate environment:

- memorization, which pertains to learning requirements for the memorization of facts, dates, policies, and other pieces of discrete information

- description, which pertains to learning requirements to provide features and characteristics of products, objects, or machinery

- explanation, which pertains to learning requirements for the use of concepts and being able to have meaningful conversations about abstract ideas and thoughts

- application, which pertains to learning requirements where people are asked to apply some of the abstract ideas and concepts to workplace and life situations

- execution, which pertains to learning requirements that have task-based outcomes associated with them.

Within each of these five types of common performance outcomes are the elements that support authoring content that targets the skills and experiences necessary for achieving those performance outcomes. Think of it as an instructional design template for writing content that is related to the categories of performance outcomes.

The sLML specification provides a framework for mapping learning experiences. Imagine that you've done a needs analysis that has resulted in performance outcomes where learners were expected to *execute* or *do* as a result of the training. You would be hard-pressed to design a solution that did not include task-based steps. At the heart of designing a learning solution based on the goal of helping a learner execute a task is a design that uses steps. A task is therefore a series of steps (or subtasks) strung together with other tasks. Designing the model that underpins what it may look like—a simulation in this case—is probably very different from that to which most instructional designers are accustomed. This sort of design is more like *data modeling,* which we'll cover extensively in chapter 5.

In this example, simply having a model that underpins a task is insufficient for delivering a proper learning experience. A complete learning experience includes opportunities where learners can fail doing the task, receive feedback when they do it right or wrong, choose the order of tasks, and so on. In the sLML framework, this is accounted for through additional content categories, such as "feedback," and allows for content to be placed in a sequence. All these structural elements are found within sLML under an "execution" category.

Using sLML to generate new content means writing content that fits inside the categories, like "task description" and "positive feedback." The sLML framework changes design by first implementing a model for design as opposed to the content delivery solution. Using simulation is a decision about how content is going to be delivered. Designing a model where content needs to be broken down by steps and feedback supports the simulation delivery but does not limit the solution to only simulations, as shown in Figure 4-2.

Let's take a close look at Figure 4-2. This figure shows the various content elements that support learning experiences that are intended to result in learners being able to perform a task. In the figure, you'll see that this model gives the opportunity to provide a title and a description for the task, but the meat of the task lies in the steps. The model enforces a view of tasks as being step based, where there can be multiple steps, and options for providing content for the individual steps, such as images and descriptions.

## Normalizing Existing Content and Assets

The other type of content you will need to normalize are your existing learning assets and content. When we add existing content like a PDF, the normalization process is different. In most cases, the content being contributed to a system described here is already locked down in some proprietary format— think PDF, Images, Flash, or even an existing Articulate course. In some cases

**Figure 4-2.** Sample Model of Content Broken Down by Steps and Feedback That Supports Simulation Delivery

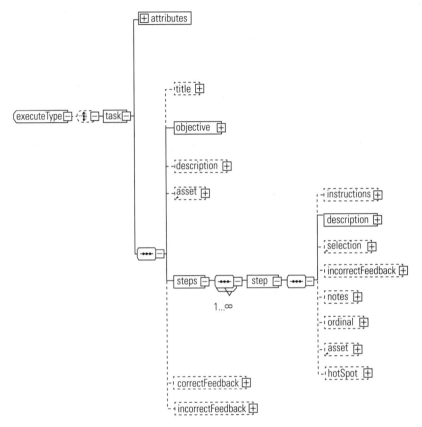

*Source: Generated by XmlSpy; Altova (www.altova.com).*

with complicated computer programming, we could extract content out of its existing format (for example, scan every line of text in the PDF) and convert the content into a structured format. In other cases there is simply nothing to extract (for example, an image). The alternative and a considerably better approach would be creating a relationship between a content file (or set of files) and content that already exists within the system. The relationships between content files can range from suitability for an audience, to audit-ability for a context, to a sequence in a program, to geography—and so on.

Take the example of the PDF. As a participant in a learning-on-demand system, I am able to contribute content to the system—just as all participants are allowed to contribute content. This universal participation is important be-cause it disrupts our existing models of the relationship between teacher and student. The learning-on-demand system encourages everyone to consume and contribute content to help strengthen the network of content available. In this example, I want to feed the system a relevant PDF. The PDF is a publicly available whitepaper on learning styles. My goal as a contributor is to ensure that the system understands the relationship between the PDF, the people, and the content for which it's relevant. Thus I need a way to let the system know that the PDF is related to other content about "learning styles," "instruc-tional design," "instructional designers," "learning theory," and other related topics and users. The goal is to help the learning-on-demand system connect a user consuming content on "learning theory" to the PDF on learning styles.

Going back to our hockey example, this is similar to submitting a new player to the pool of players, and thus we must now define the attributes of this player that would allow the stadium to draw the necessary relation-ships of that player into the context for use (Figure 4-3). For this to happen, content contributors need to enter metadata into the learning-on-demand sys-tem about content in a standardized way to ensure the system can determine these relationships effectively.

**Figure 4-3.** A New Player

| |
|---|
| Height: 5'11" |
| Weight: 210 lb. |
| Speed: Fast |
| Skating: Yes |
| Running: Yes |
| Jumping: No |
| Coordination: Yes |
| Flexible: Yes |

# Metadata

The next component of the structure is metadata (or metacontent). These types of data are traditionally found in the card catalogs of libraries. As information has become increasingly digital, metadata have also been used to describe digital data using metadata standards specific to a particular discipline. In describing the contents and context of data files, the quality of the original data files is greatly increased. For example, a webpage may include metadata specifying the language in which it is written, what tools were used to create it, and where to go for more on the subject, allowing browsers to automatically improve the experience of users.

The essence of the Learning Resource Metadata Initiative (LRMI) is a standard for communicating metadata in a standardized way to major search engines. These metadata include items such as competencies taught, types of educational materials, the age range of the intended audience, and the time required to complete the course. LRMI is very similar to existing SCORM standards, except that LRMI was created for search engines and SCORM was created to help learning management systems understand.

The LRMI example illustrates the notion of normalizing existing content through a metadata structure. Metadata structures do play the role of normalizing content, but in a way that is similar to a conventional filing system. This simply means that all content pieces tagged as "x" all get filed under "x." Although one could argue that the mere categorization of content within tags is a relationship, I would argue that this sort of tagging contains no rules about the types of relationships that some content can have with other content. This level of tagging will always be necessary.

However, other metadata structures may also be required vis-à-vis relationships between pieces of content. For example, consider a situation where a learning unit with a suite of attributes can have multiple relationships with other units in three different ways: mandatory, optional, or prerequisite. And simply because a unit is filed with certain characteristics, it is also characterized by the relationships that it may or may not have with other units with either similar or dissimilar metadata. Defining relationships this way allows a computer program to make inferences beyond the category under which the content is filed. In a learning-on-demand system, the standardization of relationships is critical and allows a computer program or web application to understand content differently than the typical filing system metadata currently being used in modern systems.

Conventional modern systems rely on metadata that surround entire learning objects (this is our current SCORM standard). Rarely do we see systems that facilitate and make use of granular metadata potentially found at a paragraph level. Learning management systems based on the SCORM standard, for example, do not read content inside a SCORM package—they only read the metadata that surrounds a package.

Most large organizations with multiple business units provide generic training to all business units but often need to provide additional business specific sections within training. For example, banks are obligated to provide a base level of training on items such as anti-money laundering for its employees. There are some business units within a bank that require more in-depth training on this topic than others.

To accommodate this requirement on a learning management system (LMS), a bank will generally be required to create multiple e-learning packages with the same generic content bundled with the business unit specific content. This creates a problem: Changes to the generic content now have to be made in multiple locations and somebody needs to manage all the various installations of that content. Remember, current LMSs can't understand the information inside a course package (it doesn't scan through every line of text in a course to determine what the course is about); they only understand the metadata that surrounds the course package.

In our learning-on-demand system, there is a single pool of content that contains all the information for all the business units. In other words, there is generic anti-money laundering content for everybody, and also content built to satisfy the requirements of individual business units. Where there is content specific to a business unit, it is identified through metadata at a more granular level than the learning object, and it is also tagged by metadata as to its relationship with other content. So if, in the case of the anti-money laundering content, business unit information follows the generic material, the business unit specific content can let a system know that it is only available if a user has seen the generic content first. Courses can be built using sequencing rules—that is, prerequisite content followed by optional content—today, but we are still limited to having one course per intended audience.

The use of metadata in the learning-on-demand system is used to service existing models for delivering instruction, but will also be used to deliver personalized adaptive experiences. The personalization happens through the metadata. The adaptive part of the system happens through analytics.

# The Analytics Framework

In a learning-on-demand system, when a user consumes content, the system delivers all applicable content based on the user's context in real time and on demand. Over time, the learning-on-demand system is able to create new relationships between pieces of content that may have been left out of the initial metadata. Through the power of analytics, the system is not only aware of relationships that contributors find between pieces of content (prerequisite, optional) but also follows strong browsing patterns among all users. Users who begin to follow patterns captured in the system analytics become matched with other content that fits their browsing profile—as with the intelligent stadium, which we first encountered in the introduction (see Figure 4-4).

A learning system that matches content to user profiles is known as an adaptive system. The concept of adaptive learning systems is certainly not anything new, but the ability to actually deliver on that promise is.

Truly adaptive systems are able to learn themselves. If a system is preprogrammed with set *adaptive paths* per audience type, and these paths never change unless programmatically set to do so, then the adaptive nature

**Figure 4-4.** The Intelligent Stadium

of the program is a hoax. If the paths can't evolve beyond what they were programmatically set to do, then "adaptive" is a misnomer.

This brief look at adaptive systems is a great segue into the analytics framework for our learning-on-demand system. As we discussed above, today's learning practitioners typically use analytics to report student progress in very simple terms, such as complete/incomplete and pass/fail. Adaptive systems use analytics very differently to make the system more intelligent, so that it can service its users in better ways. The analytics or measurements collected through our learning-on-demand system, and the systems that plug into and out of our learning-on-demand system, feed back into the system. In other words, the system isn't collecting data only so that it can generate reports but also so that it can make new connections between content and users and deliver new experiences every time it is used. Think of Amazon, which uses the purchasing histories of its users to make recommendations to other users about books that potentially may interest them. And of course Amazon's recommendations are constantly evolving as it gathers more data.

Our learning-on-demand system will still need analytics that are used for reporting. The reports available in the learning-on-demand system will not only include outcomes but also reports on experience. Experience in this case refers to the activities people do with the content (they read the content, they listen to the content, they share the content, and they download the content), or the activities people were doing that led them to the content. Granted, the experiences captured by the system are only digital experiences; but there is always the possibility for what a user may input into the system about their offline experiences, which may also potentially contribute to how the system is able to adapt. There are three objectives for the use of analytics in our system:

- Provide the necessary data to support existing educational paradigms.

- Provide data that measure the experiences and usage patterns of system stakeholders.

- Collect and report data back to the system itself to fuel intelligent and adaptive capabilities of the system.

If our system is going to disrupt current models for training and education, why do we need to support existing educational paradigms? The disruption of our current paradigm does not necessarily mean eliminating the value of what we derived from it. Before I get on a plane, I would like to know that the pilot has passed certain requirements in their training. The formality of instruction in certain circumstances is necessary. All analytic engines need to supply this information and supply the other binary analytics to which we have become accustomed.

First, the collecting and reporting back on outcomes of instruction (that is, the scores), which is our de facto model now, is relevant but is probably not as pervasively relevant as we believe. Our learning systems today provide us outcome-based reporting, yet the value we all derive from the reporting is negligible at best. Why negligible? Even if you buy into the idea that scores are a measurement of learning, they say little about how they relate to our organization's performance. Having an employee go through mandatory training, complete and pass a course, may or may not translate into organizational performance.

Second, the value of reporting back that somebody has completed training in the face of underperformance, or even high performance, is simply a data point in a case to be made about how or why an organization is performing the way it is. The way in which our learning-on-demand system will interface with systems outside itself is the measurement of experience and the collection, integration, and curation of data from within the learning-on-demand system and from outside. Examples of these may be: after viewing content inside the learning-on-demand system, users then went to visit the following webpages on the corporate website. In addition, most of those who visited the corporate site shared the topic on the following additional webpages. In other words, our analytics don't start and stop with usage outcomes; they allow us to view fluid experiential patterns that integrate the experience of viewing learning materials with experiences outside of learning materials.

Third, and finally, our system will have analytics that contribute back to and fuel the intelligence of our system. The question is, what sort of intelligence do we want our system to have and what kind of data points will help our system? In his book *The Learning Layer,* Steven Flinn (2010) notes that "information to infer preferences and interests" will help a system make adaptive recommendations and will also help build "user profiles" (p. 68). The more users on the system, the more the system can begin to make those inferences based on navigation habits, content viewed, content packaged together, user-generated rating scales, and other data points like these. These data points are all great for establishing an effective recommendation engine, but will they help a system understand what somebody who has been profiled as a novice requires in order to become an expert? The answer is partly, but not completely.

These analytics are great for interest-based learning, but need some scaffolding to handle what we have previously described as prescriptive learning. Prescriptive learning analytics need to capture "failure" against a very specific skill or knowledge object, coupled with known relationships to content that address the failure and how to remedy it. I would also suggest that analytics on failure rates among participants who have accessed different pieces of content may help our system remedy itself, for example, by linking two objects together that might previously have not been linked.

I could devote an entire book to the analytics model required to fuel a system that can learn over time. Hold onto this key point: Future learning systems need to adapt to its users, and the role of analytics in aiding this process is critical.

# Remote Content Repositories

As explained in chapter 3, a remote content repository (RCR) is just what it sounds like, a remote storage area for content that can be accessed from anywhere. As an instructional designer or learning practitioner, you may be asking yourself what the relevance is between where content is stored and your own work. The only purpose of storing content remotely is so that a single pool of content can service many different purposes. Any one piece of content can be placed in multiple contexts. As an instructional designer, you have always designed content to be used in a very specific way—that is, instructional designers and learning practitioners design content for a particular use, at a particular time, by a particular set of people. Content designed this way is local to the people taking it. This metaphor got carried into the electronic world when we began to store electronic content on local servers. Storage of learning content today is mostly based on local file storage wrapped in a standard file packaging format like SCORM, and placed in systems that communicate with the SCORM wrapper. In a learning-on-demand system, the RCR is where content sits, as opposed to the local file storage system we use today. The service and the components described in this chapter all support a very different model of learning content distribution.

The RCR in our system holds the content available for distribution to potentially many different systems connected to our learning-on-demand system. In other words, we are no longer designing content for local use. The interface for accessing our learning content can be anywhere. Again, looking at our models today, the interface for accessing content and the content all play out on the same machine.

In our learning-on-demand system, not only is the access to remote content built in, but different platforms may access the same content and render it differently for different users. Let's go back to our example of anti-money laundering training in a bank. Imagine within the training there are scenarios based on customer service where the focus of the scenario is on disclosure of information. That scenario could very well be part of the anti-money laundering course, but could also be part of a customer service course. The topic of disclosure is relevant in two contexts; anti-money laundering and customer service. Designing that scenario for multiple uses is to consider the deployment strategies beyond the single anti-money laundering deployment. If customer service in the same organization is delivered through iPads, the system should be able to integrate that scenario and deliver it within the context of the other customer service training.

Going one step further, imagine that all banks need the same generic anti-money laundering training (this is already true). Within each bank, there may be specific policies beyond the required training. RCR-based technologies allow the generic anti-money laundering content to be delivered out in multiple ways, to multiple players.

## APIs and Web Services

The future learning-on-demand system must be a member of a larger ecosystem that supports organizational performance. Again, as explained in chapter 3, the generous use of APIs and exposing as much of the system as possible is consistent with the will of the web and an intelligent approach to being a part of the larger ecosystem. As noted above, our LMSs track the simple analytics of the pass/fail type. In fact, most modern LMSs are ultimately used for capturing and exposing only such data.

The use of APIs would allow us to keep the portions of the modern LMSs that still provide value (knowing that the pilot of my airplane has passed her exams). But instead of the LMS being the epicenter of learning, APIs would allow it to fall in the background and capture that data only when needed. On any platform, APIs provide a number of benefits, including:

- They greatly simplify the life of developers by making it easy to access the functionality of the platform. Instead of developing everything from scratch, they could tap the APIs and access the functionality easily.

- Speed up the platform access.

- Make the platform highly extensible leading to a rich feature set.

- Help co-opt with other service providers.

- Help in integration and interoperability.

- Help in better management of platform security.

- Offer an easy option to handle analytics.

- And they even help ensure compliance (Subramanian, 2010).

A central value proposition of the learning-on-demand system is the communication between it and other business systems. For the learning-on-demand system to really thrive, it must be part of a distributed network rather than be an island unto itself. The learning-on-demand system will be a distributed network of services all communicating and tracking through APIs.

# Separating Content From Form and Function

The idea of content on demand, which is ultimately the basis for learning on demand, will work best when the content can be separated from form and function, so that the content can be rendered into multiple forms and function templates based on the context for its use. The goal is to remove all formatting from our content. This allows us to then create multiple packages into which the content can flow, based upon the user's devices and needs. The use of XML to mark up content is at the heart of this capability. (As explained in chapter 2, XML is a language that describes what content or data is, as opposed to describing how content or data looks.) It is also through the use of XML that we help the web understand our content.

I have touched on *structured content* and *normalizing content*. Both these ideas are rooted in the use of XML. The design of content relationships that I described above is also built using XML. Tags, content wrappers, and any other activity around defining content is all XML driven. The term *content structure* refers to an XML structure that defines, organizes, and specifies relationships among content.

Here is what a recipe for cookies (found on a website) looks like when it is tagged in XML:

<description>How to make chocolate chip cookies

</description>


<ingredients>

```
<item>Flour<amount>1 cup</amount><type>white</type></item>

<item>Butter<amount>2 Tablespoons</amount><type>melted </type></item>

<item>Sugar<amount>2 Tablespoons</amount><type>brown </type></item>

<item>Water<amount>½ Cup</amount><type>tap</type></item>

<item>Baking powder<amount>1 Teaspoon </amount><type>normal </type></item>

</ingredients>
```

XML is used to wrap content in tags that let a computer program know what the content is. Why bother? The value comes when content is able to be transformed in multiple ways using the same pool of content.

*Processing agents,* the next subcomponent in the separation of content from form and function, is a term I use for the programming code that determines how things act and look when they are delivered to a user. Broadly speaking, our system's content is based on the principle that content itself has been separated from how it appears on the screen. What determines how content appears on the screen are layers of code that are rules about how types of content look and act on the screen.

Consider how e-learning content is built today using rapid development tools. Rapid development allows non-developers to quickly enter content and use a suite of tools that apply formatting, animations, and interactivity to that content. Once a content package has been published using a rapid development tool, the resulting content is hard coded in the way it looks and acts.

Imagine now that within the tool there were multiple ways in which you could export the content into a package. Each one of those ways is similar to a processing agent and a layer distinctly different than the content itself.

Processing agents speak to XML content structures, thus reiterating the need for normalization of content. If the processing logic can't find the right tag, then it is unable to apply the formatting rules for that tag. For processing agents to work effectively, all content of a similar type must be named the same thing in a content structure. If you have ever tried conversing with somebody who doesn't speak your language, then you understand the importance of speaking the same language to communicate effectively. For processing agents to speak to content structures, there needs to be a consistent language for the agent to understand.

In a learning-on-demand system, the processing agents don't have to sit in the same place as the content. Processing agents can be built into a web application that calls content through an API.

Imagine a user who has an application sitting on her phone that communicates with the RCR. The processing agents sit in the application on her phone. The web application sends information to the RCR about who is using the phone, what phone is being used, and potentially context such as geolocation. In return, the RCR sends information back to the phone transforming into the device-specific format through the processing agent.

## Content Aggregators

A *content aggregator* used in the context of our learning-on-demand system is an interface where all levels of users can manually assemble content pieces and create content packages for themselves and others. The content aggregator feature uses the intelligence drawn from structured content (coded in XML) and from the analytics engine to display content that is relevant for a user.

Take the example of an agency representing the Canadian manufacturing industry. The agency has thousands of content pieces that are more or less relevant to their diverse audience. The portal that they have developed enables different manufacturing sectors to develop their own content packages and learning paths from the pool of available content currently sitting in the agency's content management system. Although the agency can manually assemble the content packages and learning paths for its clients, it has adopted a model where the client can access an appropriate subset of content owned by this agency, aggregate it, package it, and upload it as a finished e-learning course into his or her own LMS. Further still, the finished product can be manipulated by content consumers (learners in this case) as well. This means that an individual learner within a manufacturing sector can use the aggregator to piece together individualized content packages and alter his or her own experience of the content. Based on the intelligence built into the content, some content relationships may not be altered and some may.

Current models for bundling courses together deliver a single course as a single package and everyone gets that same package. Some organizations use a content management system where content is granularized and a content administrator can piece together different packages, but the end product is always shipped as complete, to whatever environment it is going to run in. In a learning-on-demand system, the content packages that are viewed by content consumers are built by web applications at the moment content is being consumed. The web applications use the XML markup of content and analytics to inform it as to what the consumer needs and wants.

Some of you may be thinking about the potential garbage delivered by the system if it simply puts different bits and pieces of content together at whim. First and foremost, the ability to create relationships between bits and pieces is critical to avoiding this. Content that cannot, and should not, be separated from other content should and will have that metadata associated with it. Having said that, there are times when instructional designers work hard at creating a single experience all packaged nicely without there being a need to do so. The ability to design content so that it can be strung together in a run-time, dynamic environment is a new skill that instructional designers will also need to learn—but to say more here would be outside our scope.

# The Roles of Users

Users can be both content contributors and content consumers. Within these two groups, there are additional layers of users, and a single user may play multiple roles within the system as they move from content contributor to content consumer. Looking at the web at large, most of us do play these two parts: feeding the web with posts to Twitter, blogs, and other sites, and consuming content from the same sources in moments of need. The learning-on-demand system assumes that the contributions from content consumers are on equal footing as content coming from official sources, since the learning-on-demand system is focused on the strength of the network as opposed to individual contributions. This is a very different paradigm, where there are those qualified to provide content in learning and those that need the content.

To help build your mental model, we need to throw out the notion of teacher–student, mentor–apprentice models and consider that any one user will move across the spectrum of user roles in our system over time. In addition, the system doesn't care what role you're playing at any one time, but does build its own intelligence about what you need from your use of the system as well as what others do in the system. The roles are

- content contributor

- content author

- content aggregator

- content administrator

- content browser

- content consumer.

## Content Contributor

The content contributor feeds the system existing content either through the addition of files or through the provision of links. Content is posted through a structured environment that dictates the relationships of the files or links with other content or with other groups. This content is dynamically associated with other content and is accessible based on its relationships.

## Content Author

The content author feeds the system net new content. It is fed via social media venues, by using evolved rapid development tools that allow for "content as an API" (Tozman, 2011), or via a structured authoring environment where content is marked up in XML, as well as what its relationships are with other content or with groups of people. The content generated through social media venues is immediately accessible by content consumers through the venue channel, but is also accessible as a stream associated with other content. The content authored using a structured authoring environment is posted to the content repository and dynamically processed into a package at the time when it is being delivered to a content consumer.

## Content Aggregator

The content aggregator is somebody who searches through content and packages various content sources together into a cohesive unit to be consumed by a single user or group of users. The most similar type of role in today's paradigm is the content administrator. The big difference in today's status quo versus the learning-on-demand system is that a content aggregator can be a content consumer at the same time. In other words, one can be an aggregator of content for themselves as much as for somebody else.

## Content Administrator

A content administrator is once again similar to the content administrator of our current learning system model. This role is purely to administrate content. In the learning-on-demand system, this means that in some circumstances, content contributed by a user or net new content is created, and it must go through an approval process prior to it being released into the RCR. Although the system hopes to self-regulate, the ability for some content to be monitored and controlled will still be necessary.

## Content Browser

A content browser is someone who is simply browsing content. They will use the system to check for availability of content but may or may not turn into a content consumer or aggregator. Over time, measuring the conversions of content browsers to content consumers or aggregators may turn into a valuable analytic for building in the intelligence to the system and for those responsible for manicuring the system.

## Content Consumer

The content consumer is the user who makes use of the actual content either through reading it, interacting with it, sharing it, and so on. The reasons why a user consumes content may be different, and it would be wrong to assume that it was always for learning purposes. A content consumer may use the system to retrieve content to use in a setting otherwise different than this learning-on-demand system.

Again, it is critical to put our current model for delivering instruction aside. There are no definitive teachers, students, and administrators in the learning-on-demand system. An individual may play multiple roles and watching how a single user interacts with the system should all feed back into the system's intelligence.

# Social Networking Media as Feedback Loops and Evolution

The learning-on-demand system described here incorporates social media venues and tools to not only generate net new content but also to act as natural feedback loops for content. Social networking media platforms and tools have become an intrinsic element of the web, allowing the generation of volumes and volumes of content that would otherwise come at a much slower pace if it were controlled simply by experts. The collective wisdom of participants in an organization or in a field of practice has proven to be more valuable than the master-student relationship with which we have all grown up. The tapping into curation and aggregation of content that comes from the collective wisdom of a group is as essential to a learning-on-demand system as it is to the evolution of the web at large. What the collective wisdom achieves is an evolving, fluid knowledge pool that gives you not only the latest and greatest but also the history that in and of itself forms a piece of knowledge.

My own experience in solving problems either at work or at home is that the collective wisdom found in online discussion forums is one of the most effective avenues I have. Again, seeing when posts have been placed, what came before, and what comes after seem to form a valuable source as individual bits but also as a collective piece of knowledge.

Because the learning-on-demand system not only houses content coming from "official sources," the contributions coming from social media not only grow the pool of content but also stand to correct and evolve the "official" content. It is a feedback loop where content consumers become content contributors as they comment back to the pool of content. Just as Wikipedia autocorrects itself through crowdsourcing, so too will the learning-on-demand system as content contributions come from all participants in the learning process. Social media from this perspective form a feedback loop whereby the system autocorrects itself over time and with increased accuracy.

## Semantic Search

In chapter 3 I described the semantic search. Within the context of a learning-on-demand system, all searches within the system should comply with the intent of a semantic search engine. All user roles require the semantic search, and the search should function within the context of its user. In other words, a content contributor may want to search for documents and communities that are similar to the file or link they are about to contribute. A content aggregator will use the search to find the pieces of content to aggregate together. In each case, having a search that understands the intent and meaning of the search means a more efficient search process.

# How the Components Work Together

The relationship between the components of a learning-on-demand system isn't linear—it's messy. The learning-on-demand system is constantly evolving, because its premise is to provide learning content to an individual in a moment of need, which is tailored to this need and is delivered within the context of viewing. I am not using the term *moment of need* to mean *performance support*. Planned formal training can be part of a moment of need based on the context of when that training is provided and why. Where performance support is a subset of training, representing materials used in circumstances where learners require assistance; formal training in the learning-on-demand world is a subset of performance support.

In other words, a learning-on-demand system is entirely dedicated to supporting an organization's performance, and in this context learning is a subset of performance and one way to support performance. From an operational viewpoint, the need to know anything is superseded by the need to perform tasks to the levels at which they need to be performed. The learning-on-demand system is interfaced into the fabric of a business, collects intelligence generated from other systems within the business, and ultimately provides information, knowledge, training, and other support mechanisms that deal in content to participants in an organization. In chapter 1, I described a Canadian corporation that had 350 people monitoring real-time data from its plant systems. That division's ability to address performance was incredible. The learning-on-demand system also feeds back into the organization by providing analytics on how content is traveling within the organization and outside the organization.

Rather than trying to map the system and how each component works with the others, here I try to provide a broader perspective based on the moments of need.

Let's start with a simple example. A few years ago, my company was in the market to buy a new printer. We asked several vendors to come to our office, look at our needs, and provide recommendations. While the vendor's salesperson was at our office, we would ask questions about the various printer options. The salesperson was able to answer some questions on the spot—but for some of them, they weren't. For every question they were not able to answer, they had to return to their office, get the information, and phone us back. When we got their answers, we would have additional questions that they couldn't answer on the spot, and they would have to call us back later. All in all, the sales process took four weeks from the moment we met with vendors until we got our printer. That process could easily have taken a day or two if the salespeople had the right support system.

The objective of a learning-on-demand system in the example given would be to support the salesperson before making the sale, during the sales call, and after the sales call. Before a sales meeting, the learning-on-demand system is able to support the salesperson by providing general training on products and features, contextually relevant training on specific products and features in which a client is interested, access to peer discussions and feedback, and access to what high performers might do during the sales call. During the sales call itself, the learning-on-demand system could be queried by the salesperson and relevant information could be found for answering the client's questions.

In addition, the salespeople could provide their clients with a printout of the questions that the salesperson had just answered, or even refer the client to go where other clients gave reviews and feedback. The salesperson could immediately rate whether the information they found was helpful or not to them and to their clients, allowing the learning-on-demand system to gather intelligence about what content is appropriate for what questions. After the sales call, the learning-on-demand system can be used to collect salesperson feedback, monitor social media chatter, and provide recommendations to the salesperson for additional training in which they may be interested based on the questions they were asked during the sales call. Most important, the learning-on-demand system is gathering analytics throughout the sales process and the experience of the salesperson with respect to the content they needed, accessed, used, and discarded.

To make this system work, the content available in the system had to be tagged as being relevant for situation A and situation B, or answering questions A and B. This is true for content that a salesperson took as formal training when they began working and content they might have reviewed before their meeting. Other content appeared in social media forums and as such had to be indexed against its relevance to specific situations. Other salespeople will have provided ratings and participated in social networks (here is where the strength of the network is built) and contributed back to the content about what worked and what didn't. The system needed to be able to display and deliver content in multiple formats, and it needed to be granular enough so that only content that the client needed was provided. The system needed to draw on its own analytics to determine the most relevant content for the situation, and the system was able to branch out through APIs to bring in content that was otherwise outside the system (such as the webpage where other clients provide ratings and feedback).

All the inputs of the system work to create a stronger, more intelligent set of resources for its users. Structuring content helps the system index content for people and circumstances, and analytics helps the system's users build stronger relationships with its content. All the outputs support the different use cases of the content and also strengthen the link between consumption of content and business results.

# Chapter 5

## Key Skills for Instructional Designers

- The skills you already possess that will serve you well in the future, and the new skills you will need to develop to be an effective instructional designer in a learning-on-demand environment based on the World Wide Web
- How to do content modeling—the key skill for future success
- Practical tips and tricks for designing content consistent with the web's evolutionary trends

---

What will the learning-on-demand world require from an instructional designer? What skills does an instructional designer need to be successful? This chapter seeks to answer these questions, and thus it focuses primarily on such key topics as business analysis, content mapping, and data analysis. Today, instructional designers already possess key skills that they will need in a learning-on-demand world. This chapter seeks to help instructional designers understand the skills that will best serve them in the future, in addition to highlighting areas for growth.

Keeping up with the evolution of technology is a daunting task for all of us. You might be thinking to yourself, "How do I, as an instructional designer, focus on what's important and not have to worry about programming or technical builds?" If the paradigm for delivering learning content will shift toward a learning-on-demand model, as practitioners in the education and learning industry we need to consider how to do things differently.

Let's briefly consider what you, as a learning professional, won't need to do in the future before going on to discuss what you do need to do. First and foremost, you won't need to become a programmer—XML and other related technologies will essentially be the standard under which tools and artifacts operate.

You certainly won't need to learn how to program code or create application programming interfaces for your content. In other words, the technical aspects of how the learning-on-demand system will work will still be taken care of by those who currently build technical systems. However, it will be up to you as a learning practitioner and instructional designer to harvest the technology and change the paradigm for how you design instruction to be delivered. (For background on the need to shift paradigms and learning on demand, see the sidebar.) And though you won't have to build the system, you will need to understand how we can restructure our work to take advantage of the evolving technology around us.

## How to Succeed in Business by Shifting Paradigms

When the Internet became viral, traditional media giants like Time Warner decided to take their magazines online, and they simply transferred their existing paradigm for distributing content, the subscription-based model, to the online world. But on the World Wide Web, they soon learned that their subscription-based business model was good for only a short time and quickly became old—not because solid design practices were not followed, and not because they didn't change how they were designing from magazine to online, but because their brands got lost in a sea of readily available information that was faster and easier to access than a subscription-based service.

What did these media companies learn that is also a lesson for the field of training and development? The role of media is to sell advertising. What advertisers want is a captive audience. Magazines made money because they could sell their demographic to their advertisers. So, for media companies lost in a sea of freely available news and entertainment sources, it didn't matter how well they designed—the environment took over.

Then some of the more successful companies began to evolve in sync with the environment. They changed their business model and asked those working for them to likewise change their own thinking and practices. What really mattered was delivering a known and captive demographic to advertisers. So media companies began to "feed the web" to strengthen their network, and began to analyze who was consuming what. Having captured these data, they were then able to go back to their advertisers and sell demographics.

Working with this model, media companies began and are still working toward personalized "content-on-demand" models, because delivering better content to an already captive audience creates even better demographic information and an even more captive audience for advertisers to harvest. The lessons here for learning practitioners:

1. Design best practices were followed, yet the model failed. Instead, a shift was needed in the paradigm for delivering content.

2. Content on demand contributes and feeds a captive audience—and learning requires a captive audience.

The big question is: What does an instructional designer need to be doing differently as a designer? Instructional designers already possess many core skills that will make them successful—and probably already have. Also, of course, they need to learn new, unique skills required to capitalize on the web's evolving nature. Let's look at each of these two types of skill in detail.

# Existing Skills That Designers Can Leverage

Today instructional designers possess or have easy access to three types of skills that will serve them well:

- developing business analysis skills, including needs analysis or front-end analysis

- applying learning theory to help in modeling instruction

- communicating ideas, concepts, processes, and skills.

Let's look briefly at each of these skills.

## Developing Business Analysis Skills

Instructional designers should be very familiar with the upfront work that goes into the design of instructional products. This is typically referred to as a needs analysis—or, if you have a human performance technology background, the term is front-end analysis. Ultimately, of course, the skills for working with stakeholders to discover, uncover, and translate what is being transmitted to them are really the same whether you are doing a needs analysis, front-end analysis, or business analysis (but see the sidebar on the nuances of differences between them).

# Needs Analysis Compared With Front-End Analysis

The transition from needs analysis to a front-end analysis was a significant shift and is not a simple issue of semantics. At some point, the science of instructional design morphed or merged into human performance technology—and here "technology" doesn't necessarily reflect computer technology but refers more to the science of human performance, which is broader than simply "training." The science of human performance addresses all factors that impede and improve the demonstration of skills and knowledge in a natural environment. And so the concept needs analysis morphed into front-end analysis to reflect the scope of the analysis required. Whereas a needs analysis referred to an investigation into the training need, a front-end analysis is more generic and entails looking into all the factors that might affect the individual's performance. An example given to help people understand the subtle difference here is to imagine a software company whose sales aren't as high as they should be, and that tries training to help reduce its sales force's knowledge gap and thus boost sales. A needs analysis would focus in on the skills and knowledge a sales force requires to sell the product. A front-end analysis might look to see if the software is accessible as a free download on the web. The human performance technologist is looking to see beyond the training need.

To help the training and development practice evolve further, the front-end analysis needs to be refined. A front-end analysis looks at a problem generically, to uncover performance issues in the surrounding environments. Although the analysis occurs within a business context, it is not necessarily focused on business processes or on the integration of performance within the context of business processes. The typical front-end analysis considers the business environment but does not seek to re-engineer processes as part of its scope. Whereas in contrast, business analysts look at business processes, and they look for ways of optimizing these processes through re-engineering. They use techniques like business process maps to either engineer these maps or integrate systems to work in conjunction with the processes in place. It is here where designers working to create web-based learning products need to update their skills.

Creating business process maps are very similar to a task analysis, where the instructional designer breaks a singular task down into all its subtasks.

Business process mapping is looking at the system of a process's inputs and outputs. It involves discovering what inputs currently service what outputs, and what the interdependencies of that process are. Once business processes have been mapped, as with a task analysis, it is then possible to engineer a solution that can either optimize the process or minimize the impact of an attempted solution to the process as much as possible. Including details on your business process model such as a step-by-step outline of a process, what departments are involved, and how information flows from one department to another is very useful. Mapping a business process in this way gives a designer a good model to begin indicating who will need what content when, to ensure that the process unfolds efficiently.

The skills required to do business process mapping are important to an instructional designer. As technologies and business units converge and begin to leverage one another, the instructional designer needs to understand the convergence of systems in order to apply the right solutions at the right moments within the system. It is equally important to bear in mind that the ultimate goal is performance. So those designers who are planning solutions should always keep in mind how these solutions will optimize the performance of the people working within the system.

## Applying Learning Theory to Help in Modeling Instruction

As professional learning practitioners, our foundational body of knowledge is learning theory. And thus it is our job to identify problems, needs, and opportunities, and relate what we have found to a working learning theory that can address the need of our field.

It is common practice for my firm to begin a project with a client by designing a learning model that describes the client's levels of learning that we as consultants need to consider; for example, "building a solution to help employees use a new piece of software." In our experience, various performance objectives need to be met in this situation, including memorizing functions, developing and understanding computer screens, and integrating the software into the employee's existing business processes. We typically translate these objectives into different levels tailored to the particular employee's cognitive requirements.

The reason that we identify different levels of learning is to create strategies and ways of communicating that are appropriate content for the different levels. A quick example would be facilitating memorization:

- As a strategy to help people memorize, learning theory and brain science tell us that repetition is key. The object to be memorized needs to be repeated early and then later.

- Using this information, our firm creates a strategy for memorization that is then applied to all instances of content where an employee is required to memorize something about the product.

This may seem like common sense, but there is a subtle difference in the implementation of what I have described here versus common practice.

Although most instructional designers in our field talk about the strategy, they still build a course by looking at and translating individual pieces of content. Most designers do not design structure; they design learning content. Most designers find a unique way (based on an ideal) to deliver content as they are momentarily working with the content. They do not create a universal structure to which content is mapped. Applying a multiple choice template or a drag-and-drop template is different from creating a structure that supports the learning process. The creation of structures (see the subsection below on content modeling) is the world of information architecture—a world that instructional designers will need in the future to help computer applications make sense of content. But for an exception, see the sidebar.

## Designing for Games

The exception here is in those designers who work with gaming strategies. Designers who specialize in gaming are a different breed than designers who add gaming elements to very traditional e-learning approaches—a process called *gamification*. Designers who work with games to deliver content whether consciously or not, design in the way I've described; since content is designed and delivered based on a heuristic of the game, and not based on what the content actually is. The intersection for game designers and learning experience designers is the matching of gaming heuristics based on learning levels and theory.

Building on the notion of information architecture, we must also apply this process to our business analysis for learning programs, where we are not only designing information for a singular training event but also creating something to be used in varied ways across the spectrum of performance requirements. Going back to the example of learning new software, consider that the same piece of content for which I built a structure around memorization should also account for the moment when content is forgotten and referenced at some later point. The instructional goal for the content hasn't changed. It is still something that had to be memorized. However, I need to ensure that the content can be referenced outside its initial design, which means that my learning architecture needs to account for the multiple contexts in which the information will be used in new learning situations.

In a learning-on-demand system, where the system is able to read and understand context, the information supplied by an instructional designer about the structure of the content within a context is used to deliver the content in the right format at the right time. Going back to the example of learning new software, the architecture for the content to be memorized might have included a scenario to help a learner understand when a particular system transaction should be used. However, as a piece of information that gets referenced, the scenario may not be important. It then becomes the role of the instructional designer to codify the information so that the learning-on-demand system understands when to display the scenario and when not to do so.

For instance, when a leading North American information technology company that specialized in building banking software moved its learning materials online, it recognized that its users would still need to reference very specific system transactions. Many of these transactions were built into simulations online that included context-setting scenarios about when the system transactions were required. However, those users who needed to execute the transaction while back on the job didn't need to learn all about when to use the transaction, but only needed the transaction steps. Displaying the context-setting scenario in this instance would have just interfered. To accommodate this moment of need, a different output for the content was created, so users could simply extract the steps for a transaction and move that content into a PDF.

## Communicating Ideas, Concepts, Processes, and Skills

The other skill that instructional designers do well today that will transfer over to a learning-on-demand world is communicating ideas, concepts, processes, and skills in a variety of ways. Communication is the output of an instructional designer's work. It is what comes after the instructional designer has completed his or her business analysis, has strategized vis-à-vis learning theory and approach, and is now designing the solution to match the data found during the analysis and the strategic foundation set in learning theory.

Today, much emphasis is placed on this communications aspect of the instructional designer's job. This is where instructional designers get noticed. It is where they succeed or fail in the eyes of their organizations and peers. It is also where instructional designers today place a lot of emphasis with respect to their own skills. Yet I believe that this is the skill we as instructional designers should value the *least*, because we depend more and more on graphic artists and developers to provide expertise in delivering the message. Often this is a source of great debate among practitioners: What is the job of the instructional designer? I believe that part of the problem here stems from those with whom media instructional designers have worked in the past, in addition to expectations from our organizations to be a one-person show.

In a print medium, the separation of message from layout and design is nearly impossible. Given that instructional designers have traditionally had their hands in page layout design, and that we are still working with paper today, giving up control over how something will look and its basic functionality does not come easy. Instructional designers consider themselves experts on how to design, because the final product's usability is within the scope of what they worry about. Is the font large enough? Is the layout of the page intuitive? I have friends who specialize in this, and I do recognize the unique talents that go into assessing and ensuring the quality of the design. But we must ask ourselves, what is the unique thing the instructional designers do that nobody else does? That's our true value.

I believe that instructional designers have a stake in the communication of content, but that isn't where we offer the most value. Value in this case would be determined by what an instructional designer can do that other potential team members cannot do. In a learning-on-demand system, the traditional skills for communicating messages will still be important—just not in the same way. In a learning-on-demand system, the value of the instructional designer is in setting the rules for communication—including the overarching principles for content, flow, and getting the message to the targeted demographic or other group.

# New Skills That a Designer Needs to Develop

Some of the new skills an instructional designer needs to acquire are

- content modeling

- managing content

- analyzing engagement through analytics.

Let's look briefly at each of these skills.

## Content Modeling

Why does an instructional designer need to know about content modeling? As it applies to an instructional designer, this may be one of the most important skills that will bring them from where they are today to where they could be in the future. (Content modeling, the term I am using here, is derived from the term data modeling; for definitions, see the sidebar.)

### Defining Data—and Content—Modeling

Data modeling is a skill that most instructional designers frankly have never heard of. But you can be sure that most of their developer teammates who have a computer science background have heard of it.

Wikipedia (2012) defines data modeling as "a process used to define and analyze data requirements needed to support the business processes within the scope of corresponding information systems in organizations." Let's take this definition piece by piece and map it back to what we are discussing.

"A process used to define and analyze data requirements": Defining and analyzing requirements is a skill that instructional designers need to be doing well. The word "data" might seem out of place for what we do, but let's swap "content" for "data." In the instructional design world, the data that we manipulate and care about are in fact content. Read the sentence to yourself again, swapping "content for data": "content modeling is a process used to define and analyze content requirements."

Let's now bring in the second part to that sentence: "is a process used to define and analyze data [content] requirements needed to support the business processes." The integration of business processes is a key element of content modeling, and of our discussion about moving our conventional needs analysis to business process mapping. To be effective content modelers, we need to ensure that we are supporting the business system, the processes that underpin how a business operates. Notice that in swapping content for data, the definition of data modeling connects the notion of content to support business processes.

Finally, let's look at the entire second half of the definition: "within the scope of corresponding information systems in organizations." The information system for us in the future will be the learning-on-demand system. The architecture of this system is integrated with other business-related systems and is part of the information system ecology that supports the business. What this means is that our primary target for modeling content is the system, but we need to understand the ecology of our system, to ensure the content within the system can still be shared across other systems when required.

For the instructional designer, content modeling is simply defining and analyzing the content requirements needed to support the business processes within the context of the learning-on-demand system. Content modeling is the glue that binds the learning-on-demand system to the business processes using content. It entails looking at business processes and determining the content required to support the different checkpoints in the process, determining who and in what context will they access the content, and establishing what format the content is required to be in. This will ensure that the learning-on-demand system is able to support the business processes as part of the information technology ecology supporting all business operations, through the proper delivery of content at the right times, in the right formats, for the right people.

In today's "big data" world, this means being able to search for and retrieve the information you need in real time. A content model that is improperly structured will only contribute to the problem of big data as opposed to taming it. Given the importance of content modeling, let's consider it in more detail.

# What Does a Content Model Look Like?

A content model begins much the same way as all other instructional design projects—by looking at the target audience. What becomes essential for content modeling is the understanding of various "players" who will consume the content. They need not be learners only, although the projects we typically work on today mostly involve learners. In a future state, it could be anybody who will need access to the content with which you are working.

So we begin by modeling our players. Typically, we find the players get divided by:

- business units

- geographic location

- hierarchy

- expertise

- users of a specific information technology environment.

If we were to focus modeling business units, we would likely find divisions that typically look like this:

- sales

- human resources

- plant operations

- delivery

- technicians

- other.

We may even find that some of the other top-level structures can apply to the substructures. In this example, players are divided first by business unit and then by geography. So our model begins to look as follows:

- Business unit—sales:

    - Eastern Canada

    - Western Canada

    - East Coast of the United States

    - West Coast of the United States

- Business unit—human resources:

    - Main

    - Union

    - Nonunion

Once we have structured the players, we move on to the content environment. The players are those who consume the content, and the environment is where the content gets consumed. It is here where your knowledge of the business processes becomes important. By understanding those for whom you are building content, and where in their day they will need the content, you are designing what will ultimately make your designs informed and effective. Some examples of modeling the environment might be:

- point of sales—cash

- customer service—returns

- product sales support

- patient registration.

Think of the environment as the subject matter for your content and that there may be multiple levels to identify. For example:

**Patient registration (policies, processes, locations, and so on):**
- in an emergency:
    - conducting a patient interview:
        - with a conscious patient
        - with an unconscious patient:
            - going through the process of filling out triage forms
- from an appointment
- brought in by a police escort

This structure identifies the various chunks of content that you would need if you were developing a course for a hospital on "patient registration." We have identified that there are three ways in which patients need to be registered 1) in an emergency, 2) when they have an appointment, and 3) if they were brought in by a police escort. We have also identified that the content for registering patients in an emergency needs to include 1) conducting interviews with conscious and unconscious patients and 2) how to fill out forms when working with an unconscious patient. We have simply identified the areas where content is required.

The next important part of our analysis of modeling is the content itself. Here's where instructional designers need to really shine. Here's where we dig into our roots—learning theory—and model the structure of content within the context of this theory. Let's start with the simple example used above, memorization. And let's say we need to memorize a definition.

The structure of a definition is simple. There is the *term*, and there is its associated *definition*. So, as a content model, we have:

**Definition**

- term

- definition

It is also important to recognize that the definition part of this structure might or might not be visual in nature—it might even be a combination of both. So our model grows into:

**Definition**

- term
- definition:
    - text
    - image

- video
- animation

What this structure says is that any definition must have a term and a definition, and that each definition can have an associated piece of text, an image, a video, or a sound file.

Now let's add some learning theory to our structure. Let's modify this content model to help us plan for a learning activity in a formal setting, based on the idea of memorizing a definition. As an instructional designer working on the content model, I'm concerned only with "enabling" a variety of formats for an activity focused on challenging a learner to view the content repeatedly—because repetition helps with the act of memorizing. One strategy is to make this an activity where a learner may fail a number of times and is required to repeat the activity, thus seeing the definition multiple times. This will have an impact on my content model, as follows:

**Definition**

- static—still allowing for non-activity-based delivery:
    - term
    - definition
        - text
        - image
        - video
        - animation
- active—identifying content that will be delivered in an activity:
    - term

- definition
  - select correct
    - text
    - image
    - video
    - animation
  - feedback, positive
  - feedback, negative

The data model now represents two different applications of the structure for "definition." In one case, I am providing a static rendition of a definition. I use the term *static* to let a machine know that this is a non-activity-based display of the information. In the other case, I use the term *active* to let a machine know that this is an activity-type rendition for "definitions." I built my model for the active version to support the delivery of content as an activity where a user must select a matching definition to a term. By allowing a user the opportunity to select the matching definition, I am allowing a user to get it wrong, and thus opening the opportunity for repetition. I also prepare for providing content in the form of feedback when and if a user gets the answer right or wrong.

At this point, we haven't even dictated how the content's going to be delivered. We have provisioned for multiple delivery options using a structure that will support all "definitions" and the objective for memorizing the definition.

Let's try another example—the performance objective of *identification* or *differentiation*. I often group these two together because they ultimately require the same skills. To be able to identify something means that I can pick an object out of a group of objects. This is very similar to differentiating, which is the ability to distinguish one object from another. In both cases, there is an implicit structure that requires multiple objects, from which one or more objects are "what I'm looking for." Fully modeled, it looks like this:

## Object A

∘ possible correct selection

## Object B

∘ possible correct selection

## Object C

∘ possible correct selection

At a very basic level, this model supports content that is broken up into objects, where any object has the option of being the "correct object" to select. If we want to make this model more robust, then we should consider that any object could be represented verbally, visually, or audibly. Fully modeled, using the example: "Identify an apple in a fruit basket by matching its description to the proper image," it may look something like this (note that the term *mapped* is simply referring to the idea that each element is connected back to the object of which it is a subset):

## Object A: An Apple

∘ Mapped text—description of the apple

  ∘ Possible correct selection

∘ Mapped image—image of an apple

  ∘ Possible correct selection

∘ Mapped video—video of an apple

- ◦ Possible correct selection
- ◦ Mapped animation—animated drawing of an apple
  - ◦ Possible correct selection
- ◦ Mapped audio—sound clip describing an apple
  - ◦ Possible correct selection

## Object B: An Orange

- ◦ Mapped text—description of the orange
  - ◦ Possible correct selection
- ◦ Mapped image—image of an orange
  - ◦ Possible correct selection
- ◦ Mapped video—video of an orange
  - ◦ Possible correct selection
- ◦ Mapped animation—animated drawing of an orange
  - ◦ Possible correct selection
- ◦ Mapped audio—sound clip describing an orange
  - ◦ Possible correct selection

## Object C: A Banana

- ◦ Mapped text—description of the banana
  - ◦ Possible correct selection
- ◦ Mapped image—image of a banana
  - ◦ Possible correct selection
- ◦ Mapped video—video of a banana
  - ◦ Possible correct selection

- Mapped animation—animated drawing of a banana
  - Possible correct selection
- Mapped audio—sound clip describing a banana
  - Possible correct selection

Again, we need to think about how the content may be used in an activity because the skill for identification or differentiation is an active skill. It is the active selection that demonstrates mastery of the skill but also leaves the opportunity to incorrectly select an element. In a formal setting, this requires some feedback to a learner about their selection. Taking Object A of our example, here is what our model looks like per object:

## Object A: An Apple

- Mapped text—description of the apple
  - Correct selection
    - Positive feedback
    - Incorrect feedback
- Mapped image—image of an apple
  - Correct selection
    - Positive feedback
    - Incorrect feedback
- Mapped video—video of an apple
  - Correct selection
    - Positive feedback
    - Incorrect feedback
- Mapped animation—animated drawing of an apple

- ◦ Correct selection
  - ◦ Positive feedback
  - ◦ Incorrect feedback
- ◦ Mapped audio—sound clip describing an apple
  - ◦ Correct selection
  - ◦ Positive feedback
  - ◦ Incorrect feedback

When you do content modeling, you should make provisions for multiple content artifacts that support building the skill for the content consumer. The elements you model into your structure do not all have to be used at once, but they should support a variety of ways in which the content may be displayed later on and the various contexts in which the content may find itself.

In the realm of learning content, the art of content modeling is about distilling the various experiences a consumer may have with the content to achieve his or her goal. It is the very essence of instructional design at a level that most instructional designers have yet to formally master. Thinking about content models abstracted from delivery is not an easy task, and it is not something that will come naturally right away. One way to practice modeling is to reverse-engineer a computer web screen that already exists. Look at a screen—for example, Figure 5-2—and describe the various functions of the screen elements—things like "title," "introduction," "question," and "image." Once you've done this, give the elements a group name and try to base this name on the actual expected performance outcome of the screen's content. Reverse-engineering will be much easier at first, rather than trying to build models from scratch.

**Figure 5-2.** A Sample Screen

In Figure 5-2, some important elements are

◦ characters

    ◦ the call-center person

    ◦ the client

◦ text box / play audio

◦ the "try it" button

◦ title.

What sort of performance objectives would lead us to create an activity that has these elements? Let's simplify the elements:

• We have roles, and we have tools to guide those in the roles as they interact—listen and talk.

- The title gives us some insight as well—sounding sincere versus sounding insincere.

- If our performance objective were to "identify when someone sounds insincere," would we need a "try it" button to record? Probably not.

- The "try it" button is part of doing, not just listening. Our performance objective must therefore be active.

- "Learner will be able to talk sincerely to…" What if the performance objective were: "Learner will be able to handle objections over the phone"? Would the elements on the screen need to be different? The answer is no.

The structure of the activity caters to all instances where a learner must be able to demonstrate talking skills over the phone, regardless of the specific content.

To explain this a bit further, the presence of the "try it" button has a specific purpose, which is to allow a learner to practice talking. This button insinuates talking; therefore, when we reverse-engineer this activity for its performance objectives, we need to account for the fact that somebody is practicing talking. Whether this practice entails talking with an irate customer, or being an active listener by repeating what somebody says, doesn't influence the presence of the button itself.

Another potentially important element of a content model is describing how content may be formatted. A designer may know offhand if content will be accessed through mobile devices, through laptops, and even through screen readers. (According to Wikipedia, a screen reader is "a software application that attempts to identify and interpret what is being displayed on the screen …[and] then re-present[s] it to the user with text-to-speech, sound icons, or a Braille output device—[and thus is] useful to people who are blind, visually impaired, illiterate, or learning disabled.") If a designer knows this, he or she can make provision for some content to be accessed by the different formats independently of other modalities. This may require us to create different versions of the same elements for different modalities to help applications understand when to display different pieces of content. For example, let's look at the structure we created for "identifying the apple in a fruit basket":

**Object A**

- Mapped text
  - Correct selection
    - Positive feedback
    - Incorrect feedback
- Mapped image
  - Correct selection
    - Positive feedback
    - Incorrect feedback
- Mapped video
  - Correct selection
    - Positive feedback
    - Incorrect feedback
- Mapped animation
  - Correct selection
    - Positive feedback
    - Incorrect feedback
- Mapped audio
  - Correct selection

- ○ Positive feedback
- ○ Incorrect feedback

We can help this structure support multiple delivery formats for the same content in two ways: 1) by designing entire activities that are designated for one delivery medium or another, and 2) by designing a single activity where the elements of the activity can be designated for one delivery medium versus another. In the first way, we acknowledge that an activity will only make sense in one medium; in the second way, we acknowledge that the same activity can be used across media but with changes to some elements in the different media. Here's an example of how this works, starting with the first way:

**Object A**

&lt;print&gt;

- ○ Mapped text
    - ○ Correct selection
        - ○ Positive feedback
        - ○ Incorrect feedback
- ○ Mapped image
    - ○ Correct selection
        - ○ Positive feedback
        - ○ Incorrect feedback

&lt;web&gt;

- ○ Mapped video
    - ○ Correct selection
        - ○ Positive feedback

- Incorrect feedback
- Mapped animation
  - Correct selection
    - Positive feedback
    - Incorrect feedback
- Mapped audio
  - Correct selection
    - Positive feedback
    - Incorrect feedback

The second way, again, would be to create multiple versions of the elements for different delivery formats:

## Object A

- Mapped text <print>
  - Correct selection
    - Positive feedback
    - Incorrect feedback
- Mapped text <web>
  - Correct selection
    - Positive feedback
    - Incorrect feedback

Using this second approach, I am able to accommodate details; for example:

- Different image resolutions for different platforms.

- Text that may be appropriate for one medium but not another (for example, "Click on the area where…" is inappropriate for print).

• Scrub any Flash from "mobile" delivery to ensure cross-platform support.

Content modeling has a unique capability for building web-based courses that accommodate accessibility issues without losing fidelity where it can be leveraged. Very simply, a content model structured in the way described here has the capability to support accessible content separately from the delivery of content in a non-accessible format. In other words, you do not have to compromise at either end; you can build high-fidelity content that takes advantage of the medium, and you can build uniquely accessible content that leverages the technologies whereby will be used.

Some or all of you do not or probably will not be working with technology that understands content models. However, content modeling is not something that requires any technology to implement. A content modeling approach to instructional design is about maximizing the value you bring to your organization by modeling content so that it fits into the existing business processes of your organization. At the very least, the content model will help you manage the creative process for how you want to deliver the content. This process adds rigor and justification for why you designed content in a specific way.

Before the advent of content modeling, content was designed based on a very ad hoc process of choosing a design for the unique piece of content on which you were focusing. But now, in a content modeling world, you are creating strategies for delivery based on the content model and not the individual pieces of content. In other words, you will decide what "text" looks like and how images are laid out as part of the "identification" content model. Ideally, you're not even making these decisions, so much as working on them in cooperation with graphic designers and programmers—but not all of us get to work in teams. As an instructional designer, your unique value for the process of designing content is in how the content is structured. Likewise, graphic designers and programmers have their own unique value proposition. So, whenever possible, work to deliver your unique value and allow those with other special skill sets to deliver on their unique value, so that together you will generate a better final product for the learner.

# The Role of Content Management

When internal clients call the training department and ask, "What training do you have on customer service?" it may take days if not weeks to find what training does in fact exist. We don't have solid ways to manage, organize, and track our existing content. Content may live in multiple locations or have multiple versions—and there are a number of ways for things to get lost in translation.

The role of the instructional designer in a learning-on-demand system is providing the right kind of access, to the right people, at the right time. At its core, this is content management. Content management is about managing the smallest piece of content that needs to be managed independently from other pieces of content. If content A and content B are always delivered and presented together, there is no need to manage them independently from one another. However, if content A gets recombined with content C and content D, then content A needs to be managed independently from everything else. All too often, those who implement content management systems create unnecessary layers of management for the possibility of one day managing a piece of content independently. Take a minimalist approach at first, so the additional layers of management that you create do not appreciably add to the work later to retrieve information and logically string information together.

In the case of learning content, the entire exercise of content modeling is intended to contribute to a content management strategy. As more organizations implement newer technologies and newer systems to manage content, training and development staff members need to be at the table when the organization is defining its taxonomy, which is the output of its content model—that is, the language used to describe its various levels of content management. As a learning practitioner, if you are not prepared to sit at the table when your organization is implementing content management, it will only open a gap between the organization's true needs and your functional role. But if you arrive ready to contribute to the taxonomy and have a content model in place, you will demonstrate the link between organizational performance and training and development.

## The Role of Web Analytics

We have examined web analytics a number of times throughout this book. From a skills perspective, instructional designers need to be able to find patterns within data reports and build cases for fine-tuning the learning-on-demand system so that it can more efficiently encourage optimal employee performance. Instructional designers and e-learning practitioners have been stewing in conventional reports coming out of the learning management system that do little other than provide data that, left to its own silo, can have no meaningful impact on learning or performance. The typical learning practitioner is trained to look for outcomes instead of looking at data streams—which would be much more useful.

A data stream is the flow of data that is being collected and stored continuously by systems that are tracking various behaviors of users. Analytics allows us to look at the most recently collected data points or to expand the aperture of time and look at a single point over a period. You can also adjust the lens of data points to focus on multiple points over a period or at a single moment in time. Understanding user experiences requires all these variations.

Advancing the field of learning analytics so that it can become more useful means that instructional designers need to shift their focus away from the traditional, binary analytics common in learning (such as passed/failed, complete/incomplete) and refocus their attention on analytic streams. Thus, instead of recording a score on a test, if an instructional designer wants to know if a design has made an impact, he or she could measure how often content gets shared, where the user goes after seeing the content, and what conversations about the content people are having. All these measurable activities give the instructional designer a better sense of whether the design has been effective for the user.

The purpose of looking at streams of data and the power of contemporary web analytics contribute to the cross-pollination of evidence that can suggest behavior changes in a target content consumer group. In other words, our goal is to discern how content is affecting our users. So the data received from our learning management systems today are not by default bad; they are simply too incomplete to suggest whether an organization has done something right or wrong. Adding additional analytic streams, coming from various angles of a business, serve to potentially connect what auditors want to see and the business's performance.

What are the skill requirements here? Let's imagine that we were monitoring our new project team, whose members have been through several attempted solutions to help them get up to speed.

First, choose a set of data points that detail the key aspects of the users' experiences with the content. For example:

**Data points:**

- completion status of formal course content

- internal and external monitoring of social media for conversations

- project targets

- website hits to a specific page on the website

- navigation of the website.

Second, adjust the aperture correctly to collect data around the right timeframes.

This raises the topic of data points, which refer to the specific elements that you want to look at for review. Examples of data points with which we're all familiar are "number of students who completed a course" or "average score of a module among all students." We might first look at the data points from the moment new training was introduced until the present. We might then adjust our aperture to look before training was introduced to see if behavior changed at all. We may also take an expansive historical perspective to see if there have been any external influences on the data, such as time of year, which might affect the data points. Learning how to scale in and scale out helps build your body of evidence.

Third, set up a data model that helps in the collection of analytics. When building out your data model, think about the story you want to tell; imagine yourself as a lawyer who needs to build a case for a client. Think about what story you want a jury to hear, and what the points are that will back up your story. This is where consideration of the business environment intersects with analytics. Are content consumers of a certain segment behaving any differently than other segments? We monitor this all the time in our current learning management systems where we're collecting outcomes from various groups. However, we do this more to appease our governance models than to track how different people in different environments actually experience the content. In our learning-on-demand model, we're less concerned with governance and more concerned with group experiences and performance.

Most of these skills are part of systems thinking. Going into your data and extracting a picture that will help you improve the system is the ultimate goal. Avoid collecting data for only the sake of interest and consider which particular types of data will help improve the system.

# Skills for the Future

The information presented in this chapter has focused on those skills that instructional designers now possess and those skills that designers may want to acquire in the future. The learning-on-demand system requires instructional designers to showcase their value by focusing on content and its structure, rather than the way it looks. Designers need to build on their skills by focusing on taking a systems approach to learning, which enables designers to adapt to different levels of learning and contexts; for an example, see the sidebar.

As learning professionals, our own training to do a needs or front-end analysis becomes a pivotal point in being able to advance our skills to accomplish learning on demand. It is the basis for beginning to do data modeling and for looking more closely at the businesses we need to support. Content modeling allows us to map out the various pieces of content that

## Adapting Levels of Learning and Contexts for Mobile Technologies

With respect to understanding context and layering information into experiences, the growing prevalence of mobile technologies is a great example of needing to grasp the system's role and embedding content in various levels of context. Mobile devices force us to reconsider how we design content and understand what content people need at what point. In addition, these devices force us to consider the technology in rethinking our designs. In *The Mobile Learning Edge,* Gary Woodill (2010, p. 53) says that "there is now an emphasis on user-centered learning and a push to use the 'affordances' of mobile learning to do things that previously were not possible." The training and development industry is embracing the idea of "m-learning," but it needs to stop the temptation to try to bend the technology to fit existing models of instruction.

are required for an organization's performance and the formats and modes in which the content is needed. This content model becomes the underpinning for our learning-on-demand system, which is part of a business's information technology ecosystem and likewise shares in the data being received from all information technology systems.

As we increasingly pursue content modeling, we need to fully understand how to set up data streams that will help us improve the relevance and design of our content in the contexts where it is being used. In this endeavor, assembling our data points, and expanding and contracting aperture and lens to better focus on time and data points, becomes an essential skill, because its results need to inform both our designs and our content models.

# Design Tips for a Learning-on-Demand World

In wrapping up this book, I offer four design tips for a learning-on-demand world—but of course you can use them in conventional training as well. These tips distill the material we've covered in these chapters into a handy mantra, so they're also listed in the sidebar.

## Four Tips for Learning on Demand

1. Widen the path learners travel, and allow learners to diverge.

2. Allow content to be referenced outside the initial context.

3. Build content into workflow whenever possible.

4. Don't build events, build fluid content.

## Tip 1: Widen the Path Learners Travel, and Allow Learners to Diverge

One of the greatest fallacies I see in both the academic education world and the corporate training world is the notion that we can somehow transfer a singularly planned piece of learning directly into someone's brain by using the right design. This is why we anchor our analysis and designs in competencies and skills, because we look to construct the learning material in such a way that will be impervious to individual experiences of the content and the degradation of meaning as it travels from one person to another.

Ask yourself this question, and think about it honestly: Is a training program a success or failure if a learner (or group of learners) learns something different from what is being taught through instruction? Or, in other words: I need my learners to find out how to do x, but while I'm teaching them how to do x, they somehow pick up a trick on how to do y. Is the training then a failure?

Widen the path of instruction to allow learners to digress, while still moving them in the direction you want them to go. Allow them to explore their interests along the way, and demonstrate how these interests apply to what you are teaching. Provide an experience instead of an event. This harks back to the childlike wonder and wandering that we considered in chapter 4.

## Tip 2: Allow Content to Be Referenced Outside the Initial Context

How much is forgotten after the end of a training session? Regardless of design, learners need repetition. They need practice, and they need points of reference. Designing content to be only used in a singular context limits that content's applicability to the learner's ability to consume it. The trick is to design the content so that you don't need to store and manage the content in various places for different contexts.

Therefore, build tools and alternative contexts in your e-learning courses. One thing my firm does in our courses is provide access to videos and animations in a library outside the context in which they play during the course. Our architecture allows the video to play outside the page where it is located in the course without needing two copies of it. If you can do this, go for it.

## Tip 3: Build Content into Workflow Whenever Possible

Yes, this is all about learning on demand. However, outside the learning-on-demand context, it's all about performance. One of my favorite examples of how to build content into workflow can be found above the toilets in the restrooms of every restaurant, "Employees must wash hands before returning to work."

This isn't learning on demand, so to speak; it's the embedding of information into the work environment so that it will ultimately strengthen the organization's performance. Think about the last time you built an e-learning course: How much of the information could have simply been embedded into the work environment?

## Tip 4: Don't Build Events, Build Fluid Content

Building fluid content means building bridges between what may come before a training course and what may come after it. Building fluid content also implies a little bit of the first three tips—allowing learners to digress, allowing content to be accessed outside its original context, and building information into the work environment. All these things get away from a model in which learning is a singular event. Recognizing the fluidity of content is about extending formal learning solutions past the point where they are attempted. It's about making connections and allowing the content to be part of the network of support for an individual's performance.

# Summing Up the Book

In this book, we have explored how the key aspects of the World Wide Web's technology and evolution have been affecting the practice of training and development—culminating in the semantic web and learning on demand. Being able to harness these key aspects of the web is critical to the future of instructional design for web-based learning. And as the web continues to evolve, humanity is evolving with it. More and more, the web is permeating our lives and delivering content to us that is matched to our idiosyncratic interests and environments. The more we allow the web to permeate our lives, the more entwined we become with it.

Corporate training and development professionals have traditionally focused on creating solutions modeled on the educational system. And we again modeled the corporate online university to reflect the image of an electronic school. However, because the organizations where we work are finding ways to reach individuals through the permeation of the web into their lives, we need to piggyback on these efforts and jump-start our quest to implement fully web-based learning on demand.

Given these realities, here are key lessons to keep in mind as you pursue the exciting challenge of being a learning professional in today's fast-changing organizational world:

- Focus on delivering content to learners that helps them perform.

- Help learners by contextualizing the content they receive.

- Design learning products so they can be used anytime and anywhere.

- Learners are already struggling with too much information, so simply helping them to locate the right information at the right time might be sufficient.

- Design for how people use the web. Avoid designing content using technologies that don't feed into the web's strengths.

- Become a business analyst so that you can design more effective learning experiences.

- Read, read, read.

As you seek to become a more effective instructional designer, remember that we don't design learning itself. We design the environment and the experiences that can help people learn.

# Appendix

## Case Studies of Learning on Demand in Action

---

In this appendix I have assembled examples of new technologies both inside and outside traditional training and development. The technologies showcased here are all technologies I have read about, seen in some cases, and played with in others—and all are playing some part in the emerging body of knowledge for learning on demand. Some of these technologies are being built as we speak. The common thread in all the examples posted in this chapter is their disruptive nature about how we think about content delivery, as well as their adherence to the five principles defining the will of the web. These technologies don't make design obsolete, but they do change how to apply design and what we need to be designing.

All case studies have been prepared by the organizations themselves and have only been edited slightly to fit the book's overall style. I asked each organization to discuss the problems that its technology addresses, what the technology is about, how the technology has been used, and to provide commentary on why the technology is important. I wanted to offer each organization an opportunity to really showcase what their products can do because they all represent the shifts in technology that I've discussed in this book. They are all in some way a response to that shift.

## MarkLogic

I first heard of MarkLogic in 2010. I was invited to their user conference by a client who was asking me to evaluate whether the MarkLogic technology was a fit for the vision this company had around a new type of learning system (featured as a case study later on). I had never heard of MarkLogic before, and before going to the conference I dug up as much as I could about its product. Both good and bad, by the time I went down, I still had no idea what this company did. I say "good" because its product represents a new paradigm I never knew existed and so it's doubtful I would have ever gotten it until I saw it. This is likewise "bad" because for those that have never heard of the technology, it's not easy to market.

MarkLogic is a technology that can normalize huge volumes of data or content without an existing structure in place. MarkLogic helps build relationships between pieces of content without storing content in folders as conventional databases do. One of the principles of the semantic web I learned years back is that the first step in building the semantic web is the deconstruction of everything that already exists on the web so that we can categorize and name things appropriately. I bought into this idea until I saw MarkLogic. MarkLogic showed me a technology that can consume large volumes of data and index that data based on a series of algorithms it runs on import. It then provides an API so that I can scour through the volumes of content and see relationships between pieces of content that I may never have thought existed. The use of the API to scour through data means that there can be multiple applications all scouring and sharing the same data pool, but processing that data differently.

In a learning world, this means that multiple design models and multiple systems could easily share the same pool of content and represent it differently in each model. It means that a game design could easily pull in content relevant for the context a player is in, much the same way that a traditional e-learning course could pull the same content in and represent it very differently. The normalization of content on import into MarkLogic is all about building the context of what content can go where, and what it's used for.

## The Case, by Tom Stilwell

The idea for MarkLogic began with a meeting between the FBI and Mark-Logic founder Christopher Lindblad. The FBI was looking to discuss ways that they could better manage unstructured information, and Lindblad saw that the traditional ways of managing and delivering information using relational databases and search engines were no longer sufficient. The increasing volume, velocity, complexity, and variety of information necessary for enterprises to leverage required a radically new approach. The challenge facing the FBI, and most organizations today, is trying to make reliable decisions on all of the information available to them.

MarkLogic has an operational database capable of handling any data, at any volume, in any structure. Organizations that leverage MarkLogic realize five major benefits. The first is to run your operations on big data: MarkLogic unifies structured, semi-structured, and unstructured data into a single database. This makes it easy for organizations to run their core operations on any data, at any volume, in any structure—even the most complex data structures.

The second is to be first to information advantage: MarkLogic gives organizations an edge by running operations and applications on all data, continuously updated in real time. Limitless, ad-hoc queries give executives, line-of-business employees, and data scientists an order-of-magnitude improvement in their ability to make more informed decisions, spot trends, understand what's happening in real time, and make granular decisions based upon on the most detailed operational data.

The third is to continuously make information more valuable; MarkLogic's "Living System" architecture makes it easy to expand and operationalize new data sources and attributes. Queries continuously enrich the data and the unified database is open and ever-evolving.

The fourth is to be mission-critical ready; MarkLogic is an enterprise-ready solution that meets the toughest government-grade security requirements and is delivered with the backup, disaster recovery, archiving, and high availability capabilities necessary to run and manage mission-critical applications.

And the fifth is always-on, real-time performance; with MarkLogic, organizations can run their operations from a much broader set of always-on, real-time big data.

How are customers using MarkLogic? Zinio, the leader in digital and mobile content consumption, connection, and distribution, is using MarkLogic to power the company's mobile application. The company uses MarkLogic to manage and deliver more than 80,000 digital products, including unstructured information such as video and audio clips, in real time, to customers of its mobile application.

MarkLogic uses 21st-century technology. In general, future technology is going to make it faster and easier for organizations to capitalize on big data. Today, commodity hardware can hardly be any cheaper. Processors are so fast that any speed increase will yield incremental results at best for a business. However, advancements in the software that leverages those tools will change the game. Relational databases have been around since the 1970s. Moving forward, it will take a 21st-century database to help build big data applications that solve 21st-century challenges. For MarkLogic, this means taking all of the friction out of using structured, semi-structured, and unstructured data in everyday analysis. This includes finding ways to make deployment even faster and easier than now, simple interfaces to make the software as close to plug-and-play as possible, and better ways to visualize and analyze data.

# Xplana

Xplana is a technology I discovered through MarkLogic. Xplana immediately intrigued me because they are a publisher and distributor of educational content and are focused on a "content on demand" model. The Xplana application allows its users to build personalized curricula on demand. Users can do so from an exhaustive list of resources from books, videos, images, sounds, and personal messages from other users. It uses the MarkLogic technology to connect users to these resources through the indexed context provided by the MarkLogic API.

Rob Reynolds, from Xplana, explained during a conference session about how the publishing industry in its conventional state is all but doomed. The future for publishers is content on demand, since that is what ultimately the digital experience is all about. There is no longer a need to buy a whole book to get the three chapters you want to read. The point is not that people aren't reading books from cover to cover. The point is the spectrum of choices the web experience provides for consuming and redistributing content. Providing only a singular experience of content in the form of a book negates the power of what the web can do for consumers of the content.

The changing models of the publishing industry are exactly what the training and development industry needs to look at. Having Xplana around showcases what educational models can look like.

## The Case, by Rob Reynolds

While most people know of MBS Textbook Exchange as the largest wholesale provider of new and used textbooks within the United States, MBS is much more than a wholesale distributor—and it is thus a MarkLogic user. MBS Direct is the nation's leader in providing turnkey online content services to the higher education and private K–12 markets: for-profit universities, career colleges, distance education programs, and private K–12 schools. MBS Systems supports more in-store POS lanes than any other provider in the campus bookstore market. And, Textbooks.com is a leading online, direct-to-student shopping site in the United States.

Over the years, the company has constructed a host of impressive technology solutions to support its growth, but that technology has primarily been designed to support the distribution and sale of physical textbooks. With the advent of digital textbooks and other online learning content, MBS has labored over the past two years to build out a series of new technology solutions that will support e-textbooks, public domain and trade e-books, Open Educational Resources, and user-generated content.

The challenge has been to design a single digital platform that can support our diverse client base—college bookstores, K–12 and higher education institutions, professional organizations, students, and publishers. With this diverse set of client types and product requirements, we began working in October 2009 to build our digital content management and distribution capabilities that would give us the same competitive advantages we have enjoyed in the physical product space. That work has consisted of development in six areas.

First, an XML content repository: We opted to design our platform around XML-based content and adopted MarkLogic as an intelligent, big data solution to drive our core database architecture. We have extended MarkLogic to include advanced ingestion and rendering capabilities related to textbook and training content. We store and deliver all of our book content, user-generated materials, user annotations, and virtual resource records from this repository.

Second, the information management backbone: One of our platform goals has been to drive greater intelligence around the content we store and deliver. This includes suggesting related resources for products, as well as being able to deliver suggested learning content to users based on the material they are currently reading. Our platform handles this through a combination of structured and unstructured data tools. We have an extensive set of course taxonomies (developed down to the key learning concept level) that serve as the structured data backbone of your content. We leverage this structured data to help drive improved analysis and processing of unstructured data using MarkLogic's search tools.

Third, an educational e-reader: Our market focus is education, and when it comes to building e-reader software, this presents some unique opportunities. In today's world, e-readers for textbooks and other educational content must provide the same easy-to-use industry standards established by Amazon and Apple. Moreover, they have to deal successfully with the complex page layouts inherent in the textbook industry. Finally, because they deal with learning content, these e-readers must provide capabilities for contextualized learning within the reading process. Our e-reader UI has been designed around a general tablet experience and presents a simple user workflow. We have developed a proprietary XML/CSS for converting textbooks into learnable refillable products that provide the same user experience across all devices and environments. Finally, we are using our information mapping and tagging abilities to deliver contextualized resources tagged to page numbers, table of contents sections, or learning objectives.

Fourth, online, offline, and mobile solutions: We knew from the beginning that our content solution would need to have the widest distribution capabilities possible. This is one of the reasons we anchored our UI design on the 7-by-10-inch tablet device. Our bookshelf and e-reader are available online, as a downloaded product that can sync back to the cloud, and on iOS and Android devices. This distribution capability allows our partners to focus on developing content and serving their clients. We provide all of the content delivery services, regardless of where their clients may be.

Fifth, a brandable product: The core focus of MBS Direct Digital is providing the best possible enterprise solutions for selling and distributing learning content. We partner more than 1,000 companies, organizations, and institutions. Each of these has invested heavily in developing its own brand and identity. To serve these partners, we knew it was important to design a platform that gave them robust technology and content options but also promoted their brands and their current workflows. For this reason, we designed our platform to deliver a bookshelf and e-reader within the branded e-commerce and websites of our partners. We can also deliver our digital products directly into partner LMS platforms, and our solution allows our clients to maintain their own user accounts.

And sixth, a scalable and flexible fulfillment system: Of course, our platform requires a special kind of fulfillment system to manage the different kinds of content, digital rights management (DRM) requirements, and business models our different partners require. We designed the fulfillment portion of our platform to handle scaled ingestion of XML content, an extensive set of licensing and DRM options, and the ability to apply licensing/DRM by product, content partner, or end user. In addition, our fulfillment module provides extensive reporting capabilities for both product sales and user engagement within our e-reader.

We delivered the first version of our new Direct Digital platform in December 2011 to all of our MBS Direct client schools. We will push it out to the remainder of the MBS divisions in 2012, and are also licensing our content platform to a growing number of publishers as their turnkey digital publishing and content delivery system. In 2012, we will continue to extend our content capabilities and will focus heavily on user-generated content, social relationships, and instructor tools for improving the learning content experience in their classes.

# FITT

Forum for International Trade Training (FITT) is a Canadian Government Sector Council established as a resource to help train international trade training professionals. Since it was established, FITT has designed and developed extensive curricula that are distributed through industry associations and academic institutions. They have created a certification exam and standard for what it means to be an international trade professional as well. As such, FITT receives many requests to customize their content for various clients and various organizations who want pieces of the content but not everything. In addition, until 2010, all of their content was distributed in paper format. In 2010, FITT set its sights on a vision where they can customize their content, repackage it, and distribute it via e-learning, mobile, or print with a click of a button.

My company was hired to review their requirements and provide a strategic plan of how they could accomplish this vision. Their biggest hurdle at the time was all of their content was stored in an unstructured file format, Microsoft Word. After researching the open office markup language native to Microsoft Office products, FITT was able to design a solution that leveraged existing Word files while creating distinct processing layers for the content in Word, and a tool for aggregating and publishing content on demand in three distinct formats. The interesting side to this story is the simplicity of the business issue. The time it took to customize existing content into new packages and formats translated into a cost that exceeded what the market would bear. This was a supply chain management issue solved through utilizing the web for what it was meant to do.

## The Case, by Rob Gnaedinger

Consider these real-life scenarios for the use of FITT's expertise:

- You are sitting in a hotel room in a foreign country, preparing for a meeting with a potential supplier. What is the best way to quickly understand the best method to negotiate with your foreign counterparts?

- You are preparing to board an airplane, traveling to a foreign trade show. In the rush of preparing for the trip, you realize that you don't really know the best way to seek potential partners to expand your business into this market. How do you quickly find this information so you can review it during your trip?

- You have been hired by a company to quickly provide its account managers with an understanding of the differences between marketing your products domestically versus internationally. Where can you find the best instructor materials for this type of information?

At FITT, we have found that small and medium-sized enterprises and employees of these enterprises must learn valuable knowledge and gain vital skills related to international business. Arming these companies and their employees with this knowledge and these skills is essential if they are to compete and succeed in global markets. One of the challenges we have encountered in providing this knowledge is that these companies lack the time and resources required to undertake traditional training and professional development activities. Due to budget restrictions and corporate priorities, the word *training* is still taboo in many circles.

To address these challenges with traditional training methods, FITT developed the "J3 vision." This principle is the foundation of our work to provide our customers with concise information when they need it and in a manner appropriate to their needs and requirements.

In other words, we are committed to providing not only training, but enhanced on-the-job performance support by providing information and resources that are:

- **J1 – Just enough:** related directly to the individual customer's identified gaps in knowledge.

- **J2 – Just in time:** available on-demand when requested or required by our customers, regardless of time or location.

- **J3 – Just for me**: provided in a manner appropriate to their needs (i.e., via PDF, e-learning, or m-learning).

We are committed to providing our customers with multiple ways to access FITT's extensive body of knowledge in international business—via PDF or paper (classic textbooks or customized deliverables), e-learning (dynamic and interactive websites), m-learning (dynamic and interactive mobile platforms), and webinars.

By providing such a dynamic learning platform, FITT is better positioned to meet its mandate: providing companies and individuals with the knowledge and skills they require to successfully compete in global markets, in a delivery format that is flexible enough to meet their requirements.

FITT equips individuals and businesses with the practical skills they need to compete in today's competitive global marketplace. A not-for-profit organization established by industry and government, FITT develops international business programs, sets competency standards, and designs the certification and accreditation programs for the Certified International Trade Professional designation.

# 4 Sight ECM

4 Sight ECM (Enterprise Content Management) is by its own definition an information management system. Although this book isn't really about content or information management, the 4 Sight software showcases the ability to gain access to content within a given context. Similar to other technologies presented in this appendix, the 4 Sight software is all about defining relationships between pieces of content as opposed to storing content in folders. The software also showcases bringing structure to unstructured content and normalizing the facets by which content is related to one another.

At the time I was introduced to the software, I asked the company contact whether they had an API that would allow an external application to access the content the 4 Sight software was able to find. The answer at the time was "no." However, by the time this book was nearly complete, the company was indeed working on an API. In the learning-on-demand world it is critical for applications to have APIs since the power of the system will come from a distributed network of systems all talking to one another. The value of a system like 4 Sight to the learning-on-demand system is its capability of retrieving content within a context and providing both the content and the context to this system.

## The Case, by Andrew Doyle

Organizations are faced with ever-increasing amounts of information from an ever-increasing number of sources. This information is in the form of internal documents—spreadsheets, word-processing documents, presentations, PDFs, databases, contacts, and other electronic information—and external sources such as corporate email, news, and blogs. This information is sometimes very structured (databases and spreadsheets) and often unstructured (emails, news, and blogs).

There is an expectation that this information should be easy to sift through and use on a daily basis. It's not. The real challenge is getting the information you need in your hands when you need it. Your information or content management system should make it easy for you to store, find, use, and share your information. So—whether you are looking for a presentation a colleague did 18 months ago, an email between a former employee and a key customer with whom you want to collaborate, or simply want to put your hands on that great news article from a few months ago that would be great to share with your team today—you expect to find and use information and perform tasks easily, regardless of where you're working from.

Oris4, a content and information management solution, lets you ingest, organize, index, and then actively keep your information up to date on the system and your desktop or laptop. Because every piece of information in the system is read and indexed, the right information can be in your hands in a few clicks, so you can use and share it quickly and get on with your day.

Any information in Oris4 is organized by an entity (an entity is simply a person, product, or company) once it is in the system. Therefore, any piece of information—whether a document (PDF, spreadsheet, Word, .csv, and so on), email, news item, or blog in the system—is retrievable in a few clicks with unparalleled accuracy, security, and collaboration.

Current clients are using the system in a number of ways:

- Collaboration suite and corporate memory: A financial services consulting company uses Oris4 to securely share and collaborate on projects, contracts, and news with its clients across the United States and around the world, without having to attach any documents to an email or leave its site.

- Client management and archive access: A law firm is using it to manage its client database across the firm in support of its marketing efforts and also tap into its extensive archive of documents held across the firm and make those useful to the entire team.

- Continuity and compliance: A sales-based organization is using it to back up email conversations and documents surrounding all its customer relationships, thus creating a complete corporate memory of each customer relationship. This ensures continuity in the relationship in the event of losing or replacing a key employee.

What's next? The world is producing ever more information from a larger and larger variety of sources. Most organizations accumulate and try to make sense of that information in order to achieve their goals. This need will only increase, as will the need to efficiently access information that is relevant and timely for your specific role.

People's expectations of the software they use continue to increase in terms of ease of use and the ability to hop on and find what you want immediately. There will be an expectation of a complete business picture within your company. Instead of doing a quick search on a merger target and finding a bunch of false positives of no help at all, you will find a full profile on the right person or company within seconds. The information exists, and our expectation is that the right information will be in our hands immediately—regardless of how and where we search for it.

# The Learning Registry

According to the Learning Registry website, "applications built to harness the power of harvesting and analyzing the Learning Registry data will allow educators to quickly find content specific to their unique needs. The Learning Registry will store more than traditional descriptive data (metadata)—it will also allow sharing of ratings, comments, downloads, standards alignment, etc." (Learning Registry, 2011).

The learning registry is a free resource for both content consumers and content creators to search for and link to educational resources. The learning registry provides a data analytics framework that content creators can plug into that not only stores metadata and analytics, but provides a distribution channel for that data. In plugging content into the learning registry your content can now be tracked in a variety of ways that were previously not accessible. In addition, as the producers of content you are able to use the analytics data the learning registry provides for your own purposes and display in your own channels.

Again, this technology is really showing the power of a distributed network and designing content in a way that can plug into different architectures. The learning registry is all about feeding content in a way that's understood, allowing for "viral" to happen, communicating and integrating the exposure of personal use data.

## The Case, by Aaron Silvers

The Learning Registry is a new approach to capturing, sharing, and analyzing information about learning resources to broaden the usefulness of digital content to benefit educators and learners. Not a website, repository, search engine, nor a replacement for existing sources of online learning content, the Learning Registry is an open source technical system designed to facilitate the exchange of *metadata* and *social metadata,* or *paradata*, behind the scenes. The contributors of such information include an open community of resource creators, publishers, curators, and consumers who are collaborating to broadly share resources, as well as information about how those resources are used by educators in diverse learning environments across the web.

The Learning Registry allows people to share

- alignments for learning resources to standards, like Common Core

- metadata that describes learning resources

- ratings, reviews, comments, and other annotative data

- usage information such as favoriting, foldering, remixing, embedding, and other social metadata/paradata

- resource updates, relationships between resources, and other assertions.

In 2011, the Learning Registry framework was designed, built, and tested as open source software. A beta implementation, open to the public, is available. Learning resource data (metadata) and usage data are being shared through the registry by over a dozen organizations that actively collaborate and contribute to the Learning Registry. Chief among them are the U.S. Department of Education and the U.S. Department of Defense via the Advanced Distributed Learning Initiative. More information on the project and how to get involved can be found at http://learningregistry.org.

# The Library of Congress

The Library of Congress project showcased below is a project that I was personally involved with and was a catalyst personally to begin espousing the virtues of learning on demand. It was the vision of the Library of Congress that drove this project out of the typical professional development box, into a world where facilitators could customize materials on demand to provide more personalized experiences to their students. After developing an initial release of an application that provided on-demand support for facilitators, the library decided to take it to the next step and allow the same content aggregated on demand by facilitators to be consumed by other audiences in other formats with increased flexibility.

The resulting application allows for facilitators, teachers, and students to share the same pool of content and customize their own experiences with the content across print, online, and mobile delivery formats. The application is intelligent enough to read the format you require and tailor content options based on that format. The most incredible aspect to the application is the ability for all audiences to alter activities at the most granular level. Items such as images and flash assets can be manipulated and exchanged within the limitations set by the library. This model allows the library to maintain its professional development standards and yet still offer its content consumers personalized experiences.

## The Case, by Kathleen McGuigan

The Library of Congress delivers professional development focused on helping educators for kindergarten through 12th grade to incorporate the digitized items from its collections into classroom instruction. Using the millions of digitized items as primary sources, educators can build lessons to engage students, build critical thinking skills, and construct knowledge. The library, through its Education Outreach Office, delivers professional development content on site, through a consortium of partners, and online.

Demand for facilitated, high-quality professional development far outweighs the library's capacity to deliver it face-to-face. In 2007, plans were made to build an online course or series of courses as the "Library of Congress Virtual Institute." After examining the content and the goals of the program, the library delayed developing an online course in order to invest more time in aligning the content to the staff development principles set forth by Learning Forward (a staff development association). Additionally, the content is mapped to the 21st-Century Learner Standards of the American Association of School Librarians and the National Education Technology Standards of the International Society of Technology in Education.

It was further decided that capacity building could not happen if the Library of Congress continued to deliver professional development session by session, either on site or online. The library can only serve a maximum of 25 participants each session in order to ensure high-quality contact hours. To that end, the library decided its online professional development efforts would be better utilized if it focused on building capacity to serve those already facilitating staff development. The revised goal became that the library would offer customizable activities for facilitators to adopt and or adapt to their learning environment, whether face-to-face, online, or blended.

The Library of Congress launched two sets of tools in the summer of 2009 to allow anyone to deliver the professional development content in any way they want, for free. Through the "Build and Deliver" tool set, the library uses a structured content management system to allow users to define and refine activities based on development goal(s), time of delivery, and presentation format. The other tool the library launched is a series of Flash-based, self-paced modules to support the professional development curriculum. Each of the six self-paced modules delivers an hour of content in a multimedia-rich environment and offers a certificate of completion at the conclusion of the program. Facilitators can require participants to bring a certificate to verify completion of a self-paced module before attending a session.

To satisfy the goal of facilitating online professional development, the library collaborates with vendors of online staff development. In 2011, the library worked with PBS Teacherline, the premier online professional development delivery platform to build and launch a 45-hour course. Through the work on that project and the two years since the delivery tools have been available to the public, the library has gathered information and will be improving the tool sets for delivering professional development.

The Library of Congress is working to expand its content and add more layers of flexibility. Content is currently being reworked to separate the activity from the asset. Users will soon have the ability to add the relevant sources they wish to use for facilitation. Additionally, the self-paced modules are being unhooked from its "story" environment and will become smaller, more digestible pieces of content to support the curriculum. Output of files will shift from XML to include HTML5. The library expects the new system to launch at the end of 2012. For more information, visit its site www.loc.gov/teachers/professionaldevelopment.

# Project Tin Can

Project Tin Can is an analytics experiment to help the training and development industry gather data that is more relevant to learner experience versus learner outcomes. The project establishes standards for describing activities initiated by learners as they move through a variety of learning content resources. The project, which is described analogously to the "like" button on Facebook, allows organizations to create "phrases" about activities and then collect data around those activities. I've written previously about the need for a new analytics framework in training and development that moved away from binary outcomes based data.

Binary outcomes based data is what we see in our Learning Management Systems today. It is the complete/incomplete, percentage-type scores to which I am referring. As these outcomes are nothing more than a representation of performance at the time the course/test was taken, they do little to provide information about learning itself and less than that for linking learning to performance. Project Tin Can can be used to break out of the binary analytics and empower people to not only create their own "activity streams" but also create their own dashboards for how to make sense of the results.

## The Case, by Tim Martin

---

The society which scorns excellence in plumbing because plumbing is a humble activity, and tolerates shoddiness in philosophy because philosophy is an exalted activity, will have neither good plumbing nor good philosophy. Neither its pipes nor its theories will hold water.

—John W. Gardner

---

When SCORM, a standard that lets learning management systems and the content that plays in them talk to each other, was coming to prominence in 2001, it was hot stuff. XML was a fantastic structural representation of the content that a subject matter expert had ordained necessary for her audience. SCORM's use of JavaScript for its runtime communication was actually forward-looking. SCORM solved the problem of the day (letting content work in different systems) quite effectively.

In the 11 years since SCORM's advent, though, the problems of the day have changed substantially. (The chamber pot of the 16th century was better than contemporary alternatives, too.) Learners, or put more broadly, people, don't go to a monolithic learning management system when they want to learn something. It's simply impossible for one system to be well prepared to catalog everything that can be learned *and* to know how best to present it to the learner.

By 2011, it was apparent that SCORM's plumbing was failing to keep up with possibilities of the day. People seek knowledge in different places, at different times, and they cannot be restrained by the limitations of a corporate learning management system. Web-based applications now have the ability to communicate identity, progress, and analytics across application boundaries. People don't do all of their learning in a web browser on a connected computer. SCORM's ability to track a single learner's interaction with a single browser session doesn't represent the entirety of today's learning reality.

Innovators from around the e-learning industry have been offering their gripes, insights, and ideas to the Advanced Distributed Learning Initiative (the governing body for SCORM) and Rustici Software (scorm.com), as we collectively define the new plumbing. This plumbing will be based on modern web technologies, including web services, remote authorization, and activity streams.

Project Tin Can, as it's called to this point, will be adopted by real vendors over the course of 2012 to enable different kinds of learning and different kinds of environments. Mobile devices, disconnected from the Internet, will be able to share their users' progress. Different actors, including blog authors, game players, exercise graders, and others will see their participation in the learning experience chronicled.

# References

ASTD and i4cp. (2011). *Better, Smarter, Faster: How Web 3.0 Will Transform Learning in High-Performing Organizations.* Alexandria, VA: ASTD Press.

Bartz, Janet. (2002). "Great Idea, But How Do I Do It? A Practical Example of Learning Object Creation Using SGML/XML." *Canadian Journal of Learning and Technology* 28:3.

Berners-Lee, Tim. (1999). *Weaving the Web.* New York: HarperCollins.

Bozarth, Jane. (2010). *Social Media for Trainers: Techniques for Enhancing and Extending Learning.* San Francisco: Pfeiffer.

Brynjolfsson, Erik, and Andrew McAfee. (2011). *Race Against the Machine.* Lexington, MA: Digital Frontier Press. Excerpt accessed from http://raceagainstthemachine.com/excerpt/.

Dalkir, Kimiz. (2011). *Knowledge Management in Theory and Practice.* Cambridge, MA: MIT Press.

Nations, Daniel. (2012). "What Is a Mashup? Exploring Web Mashups," http://webtrends.about.com/od/webmashups/a/what-is-mashup.htm.

Dick, Walter, and Lou Carey. (1996). *The Systematic Design of Instruction,* 4th ed. New York: HarperCollins.

*The Economist.* (2010a). "Data, Data, Everywhere: A Special Report on Managing Information," *The Economist,* February 27. www.scribd.com/doc/27555540/The-Economist-A-Special-Report-on-Managing-Information-I-February-27th-2010.

———. (2010b). "The Data Deluge," *The Economist,* April 25. www.economist.com/node/15579717.

Flinn, Steven D. (2010). *The Learning Layer: Building the Next Level of Intellect in Your Organization.* New York: Palgrave Macmillan.

Gannes, Liz. (2010). "The Short and Illustrious History of Twitter #Hashtags." GigaOM, April 30. http://gigaom.com/2010/04/30/the-short-and-illustrious-history-of-twitter-hashtags/.

Hakia. (2011). "What Is Semantic Search? 10 Things That Make Search a Semantic Search," http://company.hakia.com/new/whatis.html.

Hole-in-the-Wall. (2011). "Beginnings," www.hole-in-the-wall.com/beginnings.html.

Howe, Walt. (2010). "A Brief History of the Internet." www.walthowe.com/navnet/history.html.

IBM. (2011a). "Businesses Unable to Analyse 90% of Their Data," October 27. www.computernewsme.com/news/businesses-unable-to-analyse-90-of-their-data-ibm/.

———. (2011b). "New IBM Software Helps Analyze the World's Data for Healthcare Transformation," News release, October 25. www-03.ibm.com/press/us/en/pressrelease/35597.wss.

Kelly, Kevin. (1995). *Out of Control: The New Biology of Machines, Social Systems, and the Economic World.* New York: Perseus Books. Complete text available at www.kk.org/outofcontrol/contents.php.

———. (2005). "We Are the Web." *Wired,* August 13. www.wired.com/wired/archive/13.08/tech.html?pg=3&topic=tech&topic_set=.

———. (2007). "Predicting the Next 5,000 Days of the Web." TED Talk. www.ted.com/talks/kevin_kelly_on_the_next_5_000_days_of_the_web.html.

Learning Registry. (2011). "About Learning Registry," www.learningregistry.org/about.

Quayle, Sam. (2011). "Real-Time Data and a More Personalized Web." *Smashing Magazine,* April 28. www.smashingmagazine.com/2011/04/28/real-time-data-and-a-more-personalized-web/.

Schrage, Michael. (2012). "Tip for Getting More Organized: Don't." *Harvard Business Review,* blog article, January 12. http://blogs.hbr.org/schrage/2012/01/tip-for-getting-more-organized.html.

Search Storage. (2007a). "What Are Some of the Biggest Challenges with Unstructured Data?" http://searchstorage.techtarget.com/feature/What-are-some-of-the-biggest-challenges-with-unstructured-data.

————. (2007b). "What Is Unstructured Data and How Is It Different from Structured Data in the Enterprise?" http://searchstorage.techtarget.com/feature/What-is-unstructured-data-and-how-is-it-different-from-structured-data-in-the-enterprise.

Subramanian, Krishnan. (2010). "PaaS Is the Future of Cloud Services: APIs Are the Key." Cloud Ave. www.cloudave.com/282/paas-is-the-future-of-cloud-services-apis-are-the-key/.

Tozman, Reuben. (2011). "Content as an API." edCetra Training Blog. http://blog.edcetratraining.com/?p=123.

————. (2012). "Why E-Learning Must Change: A Call to End Rapid Development." In *Michael Allen's 2012 E-Learning Annual*, ed. Michael W. Allen. San Francisco: Pfeiffer.

Uyi Idehen, Kingsley. (2009). "Simple Compare & Contrast of Web 1.0, 2.0, and 3.0 (Update 1)." Kingsley Uyi Idehen Blog Data Space. www.openlinksw.com/blog/~kidehen/?id=1531.

Wikipedia. ( 2011). "Predictive Analytics," http://en.wikipedia.org/wiki/Predictive_analytics.

————. (2012). "Data Modeling," http://en.wikipedia.org/wiki/Data_modelling.

Woodill, Gary. (2010). *The Mobile Learning Edge: Tools and Technologies for Developing Your Teams*. New York: McGraw-Hill Professional.

W3C. (2012). "W3C Semantic Web Frequently Asked Questions," www.w3.org/RDF/FAQ.

# About the Author

Reuben Tozman is the founder and chief learning officer of edCetra Training Inc. In 1998 Reuben obtained his master's degree in educational technology from Concordia University in Montreal, Quebec and has worked in the field of technology-based training since. First as an instructional designer, Reuben advanced his career by managing production teams and product development, and finally began his own company in 2002. Reuben has been an active member of standards committees such as DITA for Learning, a speaker at industry events, and has been an active contributor to industry publications. Reuben's passion is to constantly test new theories for applying latest technologies to learning interventions and to drive instructional designers to be relevant and meaningful to their organizations.

# Index